W9-CUA-194

Leadership Skills for Project Managers

EDITORS' CHOICE SERIES

Leadership Skills for Project Managers

EDITORS' CHOICE SERIES

Series Editors:

Jeffrey K. Pinto

Jeffrey W. Trailer

Library of Congress Cataloging-in-Publication Data

Leadership skills for project managers / edited by Jeffrey K. Pinto,
   Jeffrey W. Trailer
         p.   cm.   --   (Editors' choice series)
      Selected articles from the Project management journal and PM network.
      Includes bibliographical references.
      ISBN: 1-880410-49-4 (pbk. : alk. paper)
         1. Industrial project management.   2. Leadership.   I. Pinto,
   Jeffrey K.   II. Trailer, Jeffrey W.   III. Project Management
   Institute.   IV. Project management journal.   V. PM Network.
   V. Series
   HD69.P75L394   1998
   658.4'04 - - dc21   98-12191
                                                                    CIP

Published by: Project Management Institute Headquarters
                Four Campus Boulevard, Newtown Square, PA 19073-3299 USA
                Phone: 610-356-4600 or Visit our Web Site: www.pmi.org

ISBN: 1-880410-49-4

PMI Book Team

Editor-in-Chief, James S. Pennypacker
Editor, Toni D. Knott
Proofreader, Lisa M. Fisher
Graphic Designer, Michelle T. Owen
Acquisitions Editor, Bobby R. Hensley
Production Coordinator, Mark S. Parker

PMI books are available at special quantity discounts to use as premiums and
sales promotions, or for use in corporate training programs. For more information,
please write to the Business Manager, PMI Headquarters Publishing Division, 40
Colonial Square, Sylva, NC 28779 USA. Or contact your local bookstore.

The paper used in this book complies with the Permanent Paper Standard issued
by the National Information Standards Organization (Z39.48—1984).

10 9 8 7 6 5 4 3 2 1

Table of Contents

Introduction to the Project Management Institute's Reprint Series

Jeffrey K. Pinto, Ph.D., and **Jeffrey Trailer**, Ph.D.

THIS BOOK MARKS an important milestone in the Project Management Institute's Publishing Division: the creation of a reprint series based on important past research articles from the *Project Management Journal* and *PM Network*. These reprints represent our selection of the best articles that have appeared in these publications in the past ten years on a wide variety of topics. This first edition, on project management leadership, includes some of the most important articles on leadership and its pivotal role in successful project development and implementation.

The idea of creating a reprint series came about through a series of conversations we had with members of the Project Management Institute Publishing Division, particularly with Publisher/Editor-in-Chief Jim Pennypacker. A number of issues have been driving this development, most notably, the tremendous growth in membership of the Project Management Institute in the past few years. We feel quite keenly that a great deal of important work has been published in the *Project Management Journal* and *PM Network* in the past decade that is now essentially unavailable to new members. As a result, the reprint series serves the important role of making available to our newer and fast-growing membership some of the key work in project management theory and practice. Also, with the tremendous interest in project management professional certification, this reprint series should provide an important supplement for those studying for certification. Likewise, as more and more universities and colleges are developing project management courses, these reprint booklets will offer instructors and students alike useful and highly readable leading-edge research on key project management topics.

Our plan is to develop a series of books around specific project management themes. Some of the themes that have already been agreed upon and are in process include research on project rework cycles and cross-functional collaboration, new developments in planning and scheduling, project risk management, and key management problems in project teams, to name just a few. Our goal is to introduce a new reprint book based on one of these themes approximately every quarter.

We—the staff of Project Management Institute (PMI) Publishing Division and the reprint series editors—would love to hear from the PMI membership regarding specific ideas for reprint series topics. Because our goal is to best serve our constituency, we want to ensure that the topics covered are those most beneficial to the readership. We would appreciate any suggestions you may have for additional reprint topics in the years ahead.

Finally, this preface would not be complete without our grateful acknowledgment of the tremendous support we have and continue to receive from the PMI Publishing Division. Jim Pennypacker, as always, has been a huge catalyst, cheerleader, and champion for our ideas. These ideas and this book could not have progressed without his personal commitment and help. Thanks, Jim. Likewise, Jeff Pinto was fortunate to serve as editor of the *Project Management Journal* in collaboration with two highly energetic and dedicated individuals: Dr. Francis Webster and Ms. Sandy Jenkins. It was as a result of their efforts that almost seven years of editorial work went smoothly and happily. His gratitude to them both is immense. Bobby Hensley has been a wonderful colleague and help as the acquisitions editor at PMI Publishing Division; we appreciate his input and support. Lastly, no acknowledgment would be complete without paying particular tribute to the support we have received from our spouses, Mary Beth Pinto and Holli Trailer. Although we have used the words often in the past, they certainly bear repetition here: a heartfelt "thank you" to them both.

Introduction to
Leadership Skills for Project Managers

Jeffrey K. Pinto, Ph.D., and **Jeffrey Trailer**, Ph.D.

FEW ACTIVITIES ARE readily acknowledged to be as "leader intensive" as project management. A great deal of research and practical observation points to the fact that effective project managers can, by themselves, go far toward ensuring whether a project will be a success or a failure. Project managers take on a number of both traditional and non-traditional roles in pushing their projects along the chosen path. They serve as key communicators, motivators, team builders, planners, expediters, and so forth. At the same time, they must also be the chief cheerleaders, project champions, politicians, big brothers or sisters, and a thousand other roles for which they usually have never been adequately prepared. In the project management context, "leadership" is truly a multifaceted concept.

The problem is typically exacerbated by the fact that so few project managers receive formal training in carrying out their roles. Too many of us can distinctly remember our first foray into project management. It typically began when we were assigned a project, given a rudimentary team, and told what our goals were to be. In essence, we were thrown into the deep end of the pool and told to sink or swim. Those of us who survived this first indoctrination learned a number of lessons—often the hard way—which became further solidified with future project management assignments. The greater majority of those who failed this initiation went away frustrated and convinced that project management was, at best, a bad way to further one's career. Indeed, a recent book by J. Pinto and O. Kharbanda, *Successful Project Managers* (1995, Van Nostrand: New York), notes that all too often, our "learn as you go" approach to training project managers results in doing more harm than good, both to our companies and to prospective project managers.

The current volume of reprints from past research on project management leadership includes articles taken from the *Project Management Journal* over the past decade. In selecting these articles, we sought to focus most directly on the key role played by project managers in successful new project implementation. As a result, the articles selected revolve around the nature of the project management challenge, the skills required of effective project managers, and some of the important leadership and management principles. Taken together, we believe that they offer a comprehensive and thorough look at the immense challenges and skills necessary to successfully navigate the minefields of project management.

The articles are grouped and presented in an order that may be illustrated in our general model of project leadership. This model is presented in Figure 1. To clarify the relationship between the leadership articles we selected, and the manner in which readers may integrate the contribution of these studies, we will refer to specific sections of Figure 1 (in parentheses) as we introduce each paper in the following paragraphs.

The first four articles discuss how the attributes of the leader and the characteristics of the situation affect leadership and the performance of the project team.

The first article, Albert Einsiedel's "Profile of Effective Project Managers," discusses two important issues that characterize the particularly demanding nature of the project leadership situation and then examines the characteristics that all successful project team leaders must possess to meet these demands and operate effectively (see 1 and 2 on Figure 1).

Following a similar theme, "What It Takes to Be a Good Project Manager," by Barry Posner, explores the nature of the project management challenge by identifying the most frequently encountered problems in managing projects, identifying the critical project manager skills necessary to execute the project successfully, and arguing how these skills and problems are interconnected. It also illustrates that the effective leader possesses the skills that best match the problems inherent in the project management arena (see 1 and 3 in Figure 1).

Normand Pettersen follows the first two papers with an important contribution on "Selecting Project Managers: An Integrated List of Predictors." In an age when many project managers are selected in a strictly ad hoc manner, Pettersen's article offers an important look at the types of personal predictors so necessary to project leadership success (see 3).

Dennis Slevin and Jeffrey Pinto follow up with an article that directly addresses the project leadership process. In "Project Leadership: Understanding and Consciously Choosing Your Style," they make the point that leadership styles are, at their core, consciously chosen and changeable and subject to the unique nature of the problem and characteristics of leaders and followers. Successful project managers are those capable of managing their own transition from one leadership style to another as circumstances dictate (see 1, 2, 3 and 4).

The next three articles focus on improving project leadership through skill assessment and training.

The fifth article, "Developing Project Management Skills," by Hans Thamhain, looks at the specific skills project managers need to possess, breaking them down into leadership, technical, and administrative. He then presents twelve alternative skill development methods and assesses the effectiveness of each method. In conclusion, he synthesizes this information to offer some important managerial implications for developing project management skills to their highest potential (see 5).

"Learning to Lead, to Create Quality, to Influence Change in Projects," by Lee Peters and John Homer, offers key insights into the central problem of

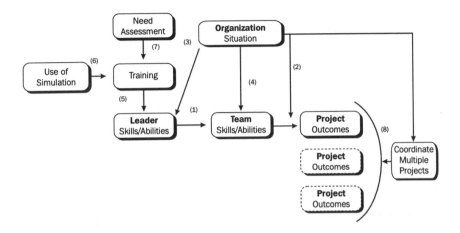

Figure 1

developing project managers: how to produce a "mission-capable project manager in a relatively short time." These authors make the argument that the use of simulation is effective in developing critical project management skills quickly because it allows a high feedback cycle and creates a relatively low-risk learning environment. Their article draws on research from the quality movement and offers important practical lessons and implications from their own experiences (see 6).

The seventh article, "Situational Leadership in a Project/Matrix Environment," by Nicholas DiMarco, Jane Goodson, and Henry Houser, describes a situational approach to assessing the need for leadership training. They identify fifteen specific leadership aspects that can be assessed and subsequently used to design and focus their management development efforts. Their study is based on a sample of project managers, functional area managers, and their employees in a project-based engineering firm. They outline key dimensions of effective project managers and offer some suggestions on how to improve the skill set of project leaders for future success (see 7).

The next article shifts the focus to the project team and addresses how to enhance the project leader's ability to develop and build the team. "The Project Manager as Team Builder: Creating an Effective Team," by Lawrence Todryk, explores one of the critical responsibilities that all project managers must face: the ability to effectively mold a disparate group of individuals from various functional backgrounds into an effective team. This article explores the characteristics of effective teams and the steps necessary to turn people whose primary loyalties lie with their functional affiliations into a potent, unified project team (see 1 and 4).

The final set of articles discusses leading the project team in the context of the larger organization.

Project leaders must continually work to bridge the gap between their own activities and top management's concerns. In their article, "Design of Project Management Systems from Top Management's Perspective," Christian Navarre and Jean-Louis Schaan provide the results of some important research into the process of effectively blending the problems of single project management with the concerns of top management, trying to successfully balance a portfolio of projects (see 8).

The final article, "Organizational Culture and Project Leader Effectiveness," by Michael Elmes and David Wilemon, puts the leadership challenge into its larger context—effectively managing with an understanding of the unique relationship an organization's culture has with the culture of the project team. The authors present a typology of cultures to help the project manager classify the cultures in their situations, and they provide four generic "influence strategies" to assist project managers in interacting effectively with the identified cultures. The authors argue that unless we fully understand the unique culture of the firm, it is impossible to lead effectively, influence correctly, or manage the project for future success (see 3 and 4 on Figure 1).

Profile of Effective Project Managers

Albert A. Einsiedel, Jr., Ph.D., University of Alberta

Project Management Journal 18, no. 5 (December 1987)

WHY ARE SOME individuals more consistently successful as project managers than others? Do they perform more effectively because they possess certain traits and competencies—the "right stuff" for managing projects—and, if so, what are these qualities and abilities?

The success or failure of most managers depends on a wide variety of factors, some of which have little or nothing to do with the manager's personal ability or motivation. For example, it is conceivable that particular individuals may have been assigned to "manage" a project over which they have very little real influence. Such a project is destined to succeed or fail depending on a variety of factors, many of which may have very little to do with what the manager does. These "leader-proof" projects are similar to some man-machine systems that are "operator-proof" or to training systems that are "instructor-proof." Situational factors (for example, the ease or difficulty of achieving the project's scope and deadline) rather than leadership competencies are what determine the outcome of these projects.

At the other extreme are "leader-sensitive" projects. Their outcome depends heavily on the project manager's performance, which, in turn, is contingent on the manager's competence and motivation. Often the project managers themselves are the project champions and, in extreme cases, the personification of the project. Their style, whether effective or not, distinguishes the project. For better or worse, they represent the project's primary human asset or liability.

For projects that fall closer to the leader-sensitive end of the continuum, it is important to select the individual most suitably matched to the requirements of the project leadership situation. One important assumption that is made is that not everyone is equally suited to manage projects, and certain individuals are more likely to contribute significantly to a project's success than others. A random process of selecting project managers for these projects may produce a good match. Rational decision-makers, however, are apt to prefer a more systematic approach, such as sound recruitment, selection, and training, in order to maximize the probability of a good fit. Of course, an alternative is to "engineer" the leadership environment to match the manager's characteristics (4), a method that is viable under certain conditions.

Characteristics of the Project Leadership Situation

Projects are relatively unique solutions to extraordinary organizational problems for which the traditional bureaucratic responses are considered too slow or inflexible to be effective (3). Many organizations employ project management because there are advantages in having a "custom-designed" project unit that is sufficiently responsive, flexible, autonomous, and effective in coordinating activities of different specialists and diverse groups.

There are two characteristics of project situations that are particularly challenging for the project manager: one concerns the organizational structure, and the other concerns the decision-making environment. These characteristics do not necessarily describe all project situations, nor are they permanent, even when they do occur for any given project.

1. Trend Toward Adhocracy: Many project organizations take the form of adhocracies, or temporary work organizations. Adhocracies, such as task forces, are generally viewed as effective in fostering innovation. They tend to thrive most effectively in fluid, high-risk environments and are relatively more vulnerable than bureaucracies. Organizations in a competitive environment, where creative and timely action spells the difference between success and failure, have made adhocracies useful adjuncts to existing bureaucracies. They have cultivated entrepreneurial organizational values and fostered an environment that is conducive to innovation (6) (11).

Some project activities are relatively confined to specific individuals or well-defined organizational units, such as research and development departments. Others rely heavily on a combination of resources from different individuals and organizations. When many activities call for the integrating of resources, the organization establishes ad hoc project teams, or task forces, in the form of matrix organizations. These types of project organizations feature combinations of personnel drawn from a number of sources, for example, functional departments within the organization and, for some activities, outside the organization, as well as contractors or external consultants. Some matrix organizations are relatively permanent, while others shift from one phase of the project to the next (10).

In matrix organizations, many of the resources required to complete the project are often controlled by the functional managers rather than by the project manager (12). For example, the specialists, technology, and materials may be under the direct control of the functional managers. The project manager must bargain and negotiate in order to access the appropriate resources. Information and technical expertise are other examples of scarce resources around which organizational power is organized. In many cases, the project manager possesses insufficient amounts of the technical expertise required to make important decisions. To add to the difficulty posed by these dependencies, the project situation often changes rapidly, whether by design or by circumstance, and does not permit routine to set in. The major disadvantage of the matrix organization is its tendency to create confusion, foster power struggles, and generate stress associated with role ambiguity, role conflict, and role erosion (1). It is not surprising in such a situation to discover that much of a manager's time and energy is devoted to activities directly related to gaining, maintaining, or using power (7) (9).

2. Limited Area of Rationality: Although careful planning during the project's earlier developmental stages and the establishment of effective project control systems can reduce management problems in the downstream stages, new information and unexpected developments often present difficulties that must be addressed by the project manager and the project team. Project leaders must facilitate effective decision-making, a task that is made onerous when there is a paucity of good information, time, and creative energy.

The typical situation faced by a project manager is one that places certain limits on the manager's knowledge and information, thus restricting the "area of rationality" that guides the manager and the project staff's actions. Herbert Simon (14, p. 24) noted that:

> the individual can be rational in terms of the organization's goals only to the extent that he is **able** to pursue a particular course of action, he has a correct conception of the **goal** of his action, and he is correctly **informed** about the conditions surrounding his action. Within the boundaries laid down by these factors his choices are rational-goal-oriented.

The behavior of project personnel—and especially the project manager—is determined by limited alternatives, values, skills, and knowledge relevant to the project's goals. In some cases, rational decision-making gives way to "garbage can" decisions, such as occurs when available solution alternatives, decision participants, and resources define what problems will be solved rather than the other way around (2).

Characteristics of an Effective Project Leader

Many project managers have dual roles: manager and principal content expert. Most are primarily managers and coordinate a number of experts. They act in the role of "marginalists" who must make sure that decisions are made at the proper time, within the proper framework or expertise, and by the proper people. "Project managers," Sayles (13) observed, "function as bandleaders who pull together their players, each a specialist with individual score and internal rhythm. Under the leader's direction, they all respond to the same beat" (13, p. 194).

Project managers, such as brand managers in consumer-goods firms, perform the function of an "integrating manager" when they are assigned the formal authority to coordinate mutual adjustments required in matrix organizations. They must be skillful at sharing power and have the ability "to stand between conflicting groups and gain the acceptance of both without being absorbed by either" (10, p. 84).

There are at least five related qualities that are essential to be able to perform these roles effectively.

1. Credibility: Is the project manager taken seriously? Does this individual have credibility? Credibility refers to a combination of the manager's expertise and trustworthiness in the eyes of the project's clients, the manager's superiors, functional managers, subordinates, external consultants, and contractors. Specifically, it is a significant asset to a project manager to have the specialized technical education or training, as well as a track record of successful project management, that is relevant to the current project. For example, an experienced petrochemical engineer would be perceived as having greater credibility than non-engineers in petrochemical engineering projects. One who has a reputation for successfully managing similar projects would be taken more seriously than one who has not managed or worked on related projects. In addition, the manager must be perceived as being dependable and honest and should not appear to have dysfunctional ulterior motives. The project manager must be sufficiently credible to be able to contribute effectively to the design of the project, exercise effective control, and negotiate and bargain effectively.

2. Creative Problem-Solver: Is the project manager skilled at problem analysis and identification, in facilitating the emergence of creative solutions, and in arriving at optimal solutions? When, under severe time constraints, optimizing must give way to satisfying decision-making, can the project manager just as effectively formulate correct and acceptable decisions? Often, the adhocracy must quickly improvise a solution but cannot strictly "go by the book" and employ established and standardized bureaucratic procedures. The willingness to take risk and attempt innovative approaches can mean the difference between success or failure in determining the best tradeoffs between quality, cost, and time.

3. Tolerance for Ambiguity: Is the project manager adversely affected by ambiguous and uncertain situations? One of the most frequently cited characteristics of projects is ambiguity. Some projects have ambiguous ends, goals, or objectives; it is not clear precisely what results the project intends to achieve. Some projects have ambiguous means; it is not clear what resources are available or have been authorized, or what methodology or approach is most suitable to achieve the project ends. Planning and control systems help only to the extent that project planners have much of the quality information needed to specify and forecast what is feasible. When quality information is not available when needed, there is a tendency to either overestimate or underestimate costs, activity duration, and personnel capabilities. Some project planners deliberately "under plan" and leave room for discretionary decisions to be made during the implementation phase when the "realities" of the project become manifest. Others "over plan" in spite of the lack of quality information, often giving an illusion of predictability and control when, in fact, there is much uncertainty. This is sometimes done deliberately to induce realities to conform to plans. More often, I suspect, they are used merely to create a favorable impression on clients and superiors.

Individuals who are unable to function effectively under conditions of ambiguity and uncertainty are apt to find most project situations to be stressful. Since they often cannot "go by the book" and must, instead, improvise as they go along, it is helpful for project managers to develop or to possess a high degree of tolerance for ambiguity, a characteristic that requires a high degree of cognitive complexity and maturity. For many projects, the manager must deal with a continuous string of minor and major issues or crises. An individual who is not able to adapt to rapid and unpredictable changes is likely to experience chronic stress and, eventually, burnout. Those who do, on the other hand, are conditioned by the successful experience and are subsequently able to resist even greater stresses.

4. Flexible Management Style: Does the leadership situation change frequently, and can the project manager's leadership style change with the requirements of the shifting situation? Situational leadership principles suggest that managers who possess a wide repertoire of management styles have an advantage over managers who have a relatively narrow range of styles (5). When the situation calls for task-oriented leadership behavior (e.g., clarifying priorities, deadlines, responsibilities, and standards), as is often the case in the earlier stages of a project, a project manager must be both willing and able to provide task structure and be an assertive leader. When the project team has developed sufficient teamwork, expertise, and motivation, and the need for task-oriented behavior has diminished, the leader should switch to a less task-oriented style. To persist in applying the same dose of task-oriented behavior that worked earlier may have an adverse effect on the morale and performance of the "task mature" team.

5. Effective Communication Skills: Having effective communication skills is an asset in many managerial jobs, but it is especially critical in project leadership roles. The project manager is expected to be competent in receiving, processing, and transmitting complex messages to and from clients, superiors, functional managers, subordinates, contractors, external consultants, and, in some projects, the media and the public. The success of the project often hinges on how well the project manager handles information whether it is technical, legal, administrative, or interpersonal in nature.

An effective manager must be a good observer, an excellent listener, and must attend to important details while being conscious of the ever-present danger of information overload. In many cases, deadline pressures and demands for immediate action preclude careful information gathering, analysis, and documentation, let alone communicating all information or decisions to all parties concerned. Effective and efficient communication skills are necessary to avoid costly mistakes.

The management of numerous dependency relationships requires willingness and the ability to communicate frequently, effectively, and efficiently. Sayles (13) suggests that matrix structures are for organizations that are prepared to resolve their conflicts through informal negotiations among equals rather than through recourse to formal authority. If the organization is not sufficiently mature, effective informal communication may not occur easily. Many decisions that have to be made and implemented on the basis of an informal understanding between parties, rather than on a more formal agreement or contract, may be adversely affected.

Developing the Right Stuff

The importance of obtaining a proper match between the individual's characteristics and the role requirements is directly related to the degree to which the project is leader sensitive. How this can be achieved is a matter of preference. Fiedler (4) argued that it is often easier to change the situation to match the leader's style and personality. Hersey and Blanchard (5) and Simon (14) are more optimistic that knowledge and skills can be learned to give the manager a wider range of alternative approaches.

Project managers who have the "right stuff" for effective leadership probably acquired these competencies by managing projects through trial and error, often with some help from mentors and through formal training. In addition to intuition, commonsense, and a sense of confidence, they probably also have a healthy measure of the need to achieve and the need to acquire and use organizational power (8). Success was probably experienced in modest amounts in earlier projects but with more experience and practice, mastery of the project environment evolved into a sophisticated and esoteric art form.

Project managers are like many jazz musicians who, more so than their "classically trained" bureaucratic counterparts, are adept at doing improvisations, playing to their audience, and varying the tempo to match the mood of the situation. Both can be effective in their respective roles. Some can be effective in either role.

References

1. Davis, S.M., and P.R. Lawrence. 1978. Problems of Matrix Organizations. *Harvard Business Review* (May–June 1978): 131–142.

2. Einsiedel, A.A., Jr. 1983. Decision-Making and Problem Solving Skills: The Rational versus the Garbage Can Models of Decision-Making. *Project Management Quarterly* 14: 52–57.

3. ———. 1984. *Improving Project Management*. Boston, Massachusetts: International Human Resources Development Corporation.

4. Fiedler, F.E. 1965. Engineer the Job to Fit the Manager. *Harvard Business Review* 43: 115.

5. Hersey, P., and K.H. Blanchard. 1977. *Management of Organizational Behavior*. Englewood Cliffs, N.J.: Prentice-Hall.

6. Knight, R.M. 1985–1986. Corporate Innovation and Entrepreneurship in Canada. *Business Quarterly* 5, no. 4 (Winter): 83–90.

7. Kotter, J.P. 1978. Power, Success, and Organizational Effectiveness. *Organizational Dynamics* (Winter): 27–40.

8. McClelland, D. C., and D.H. Burnham. 1976. Power Is the Great Motivator. *Harvard Business Review* (March–April): 100–110.

9. Mintzberg, H. 1973. *The Nature of Managerial Work*. New York: Harper & Row.

10. ———. 1983. *Structures in Five: Designing Effective Organizations*. Englewood Cliffs, N.J.: Prentice-Hall.

11. Peters, T.J., and R.H. Waterman, Jr. 1982. *In Search of Excellence*. New York: Harper & Row.

12. Robbins, S.R. 1983. *Organizational Theory*. Englewood Cliffs, N.J.: Prentice-Hall.

13. Sayles, L.R. 1979. *Leadership: What Effective Managers Really Do . . . and How They Do It*. New York: McGraw-Hill.

14. Simon, H.A. 1976. *Administrative Behavior*. New York: The Free Press

What It Takes to Be a Good Project Manager

Barry Z. Posner, Santa Clara University

Project Management Journal 18, no. 1 (March 1987)

S ELECTING A GOOD project manager is not a simple task. Being an effective project manager is an ongoing challenge. The complex nature and multifaceted range of activities involved in managing projects precludes easily identifying managerial talent and continually stretches the capabilities of talented project managers. Two seemingly contradictory viewpoints have been advanced about what is required to be a good project manager.

One perspective prescribes a set of *personal characteristics* necessary to manage a project (1). Such personal attributes include aggressiveness, confidence, poise, decisiveness, resolution, entrepreneurship, toughness, integrity, versatility, multidisciplinary, and quick thinking.

However, Daniel Rowan (2) maintains that it would take an extraordinary individual to have all of these critical personal characteristics. A more practical solution, he suggests, would be to determine the *critical problems* faced by project managers and select a person who can handle such difficulties. The shortcoming with this second perspective, argue those like Michael Badaway (3), is that the primary problems of project managers are really not technical ones. The reason managers fail at managing projects, he contends, is because they lack critical organization and management skills.

Scholars like Rowan and Badaway—as well as practitioners—may actually be raising different issues. On the one hand, good project managers understand the critical problems that face them and are prepared to deal with them. On the other hand, managing projects well requires a set of particular attributes and skills. But, are these two viewpoints really at odds with one another? In this study they were discovered to be two sides of the *same* coin!

Study of Project Manager Problems and Skills

Questionnaires were completed by project managers during a nationwide series of project management seminars. Project managers attending these seminars came from a variety of technology-oriented organizations. Responses to the survey instrument were both voluntary and confidential.

Information about the respondents and the nature of their projects was collected. The typical project manager was a thirty-seven-year-old male, had nine people reporting to him, and was responsible for a small- to moderate-sized project within a matrix organization structure. More specifically, there were 189 men and ninety-eight women in the sample (N = 287), and their ages ranged from twenty-two to sixty years of age (X = 37.4, S.D. = 8.3). Fifty-six percent indicated that they were the formal managers of the project. The size of their immediate project group ranged from two to over one hundred people (median = 8.9). Fifty-nine percent reported that they worked primarily on small projects (involving few people or functions, with a short time horizon). More than 63 percent indicated that they were working within a matrix organization structure. No information was collected about the specific nature (e.g., new product development, research and development, MIS) of their projects.

Two open-ended questions were asked. (Their order was randomized). The first asked about the skills necessary to be a successful project manager. The second question investigated the most likely problems encountered in managing projects. Responses to these questions were analyzed by content. Content analysis is a systematic approach to data analysis, resulting in both qualitative assessments and quantitative information. Each respondent comment was first coded and then recorded several times, as patterns of responses became apparent. The two questions were:

- What factors or variables are **most** likely to cause you problems in managing a project?
- What **personal** characteristics, traits, or skills make for "above average" project managers? What specific behaviors, techniques, or strategies do "above average" project managers use (or use better than their peers)?

Problems in Managing Projects

There were nearly nine hundred statements about what factors or variables created "problems" in managing a project. Most of these statements could be clustered into eight categories as shown in Table 1.

The issue most frequently mentioned, as causing problems in managing a project, was inadequate resources. "No matter what the type or scope of your project," wrote one engineering manager, "if insufficient resources are allocated to the project, you have to be a magician to be successful." Not having the necessary budget or personnel for the project was a frequent complaint. However, the specific resource of *time*—and generally the lack thereof—was mentioned just about as often as the general inadequate resource lament. Typically, the problem of time was expressed as "having to meet unrealistic deadlines."

Project Management Problems

Resources inadequate (69)
Meeting ("unrealistic") deadlines (67)
Unclear goals/direction (63)
Team members uncommitted (59)
Insufficient planning (56)
Breakdowns in communication (54)
Changes in goals and resources (42)
Conflicts between departments or functions (35)

Table 1

That resources are inadequate is caused by many factors, not the least of which being that resources are generally limited and costly. Before this hue is dismissed by veteran project managers as just so much bellyaching—"after all, there are never enough resources"—it is important to examine the cause(s) of this problem. Respondents pointed out that resource allocation problems were usually created by senior management's failure to be clear about project objectives, which, in turn, resulted in poor planning efforts. These two problems—lack of clear goals and effective planning—were specifically mentioned by more than 60 percent of the respondents. It is painfully obvious that vague goals and insufficient planning lead to mistakes in allocating the resources needed by project managers.

The three most significant problems reported by first-line research, development, and engineering supervisors in Lauren Hitchcock's (4) study parallel those identified by project managers. He found "insufficient definition of policy from top downward, how to define the goal of a problem, and budgeting and manpower assignments" to be the major problems confronting supervisors. It remains true that senior management needs to articulate clearly where the project should be going, why, and what it expects from project personnel.

When project goals are not clear, it is difficult (if not impossible) to efficiently plan the project. The lack of planning contributes directly to unrealistic resource allocations and schedules. People assigned to the project are unlikely, therefore, to energetically commit to the endeavor. The lack of commitment (and poor motivation) among project personnel was reported as emerging more from the problems already mentioned than to issues associated with the project's technology or organizational structure (e.g., matrix form).

The communication breakdowns (problems), which occur during the life of a project, were often referred to as "inevitable." These breakdowns occur as a result of the ambiguity surrounding the project but also result from difficulties in coordinating and integrating diverse perspectives and personalities. The project manager's challenge is to handle communication breakdowns as they arise rather than being able to predict (and control) communication problems before they happen.

How the problems confronting project managers were interrelated is exemplified by how frequently problems of communication and dealing with conflicts were linked by respondents. The linkage between these two issues was demonstrated in statements like: "My problem is being able to effectively communicate with people when we disagree over priorities," and, "Conflicts between departments end up as major communication hassles." Conflicts between departments were also linked to earlier problems of poor goal setting and planning.

Managing changes (e.g., in goals, specifications, resources, and so on) contributed substantially to project management headaches. This was often mentioned as "Murphy's Law," highlighting the context or environment in which project management occurs. Planning cannot accurately account for future possibilities (or better yet, unknowns). Interestingly, less than one in ten project managers mentioned directly a "technological" factor or variable as significantly causing them problems in managing a project.

Project Manager Skills

The second issue investigated was what project manager skills—traits, characteristics, attributes, behaviors, and techniques—make a difference in successfully managing projects. Most respondents easily generated four to five items that they believed made the difference between average and superior project performance. The result was nearly 1,400 statements. These statements were summarized into six skill areas as shown in Table 2. Several factors within each are highlighted.

Eighty-four percent of the respondents mentioned "being a good communicator" as an essential project manager skill. Being persuasive or being able to sell one's ideas was frequently mentioned as a characteristic of a good communicator within the project management context. Many people also cited the importance of receiving good information or having good listening skills. As one systems engineer exclaimed: "The good project managers manage not by the seat of their pants but by the soles of their feet!"

Organizational skills represented a second major set of competencies. Characteristics included in this category were planning and goal-setting abilities, along with the ability to be analytical. The ability to prioritize—captured in the phrases "stays on track" and "keeps the project goals in perspective"—was also identified as significant.

While successful project managers were viewed as good problem solvers, what really differentiated them from their so-so counterparts was their problem-*finding* ability. Because of their exceptional communication skills, goal clarity, and planning, effective project managers were aware of issues *before* they became

Project Management Skills

Communication Skills (84)
    Listening
    Persuading

Organizing Skills (75)
    Planning
    Goal-Setting
    Analyzing

Team Building Skills (72)
    Empathy
    Motivation
    Esprit de Corps

Leadership Skills (68)
    Sets Example
    Energetic
    Vision (big picture)
    Delegates
    Positive

Coping Skills (59)
    Flexibility
    Creativity
    Patience
    Persistence

Technological Skills (46)
    Experience
    Project Knowledge

Table 2

problems. Problem finding gave them greater degrees of freedom enabling them to avoid being seriously sidetracked by problems caused by unforeseen events.

The important team building skills involved developing empathic relationships with other members of the project team. Being sensitive to the needs of others, motivating people, and building a strong sense of team spirit were identified as essential for effectively managing a project. "The best project managers use a lot of **we** statements in describing the project," wrote one computer programmer. Being clear about the project's objectives and subsequently breaking down the project into its component parts (e.g., schedules) helped project participants to understand their interdependencies and the need for teamwork.

Several different attributes and behaviors were cataloged under leadership skills. These included setting a good example, seeing the big picture, being enthusiastic, having a positive outlook, taking initiative, and trusting people. Having a vision is closely related to goal clarity (which was included as an organizational skill). The leadership component of this competency was best expressed by one financial analyst as "the ability to see the forest through the trees."

Since, as is often lamented, the only constant in managing a project is change, successful project managers require coping or stress management skills. Respondents indicated that both flexibility and creativity were involved in effectively dealing (or coping) with change, as were patience and persistence. What project managers experience are generally high levels of stress. How well they handle stress ("grace under pressure") significantly affects their eventual success or failure.

The final cluster of skills was labeled "technological." Successful project managers were seen as having relevant experience or knowledge about the technology required by the project. Seldom, however, were effective project managers seen as the technological "experts." Indeed, expertise was often felt to be detrimental because it decreased flexibility and the willingness to consider alternative perspectives. Project managers do need to be sufficiently well versed in the technology to be able to ask the right questions because, as one senior military officer pointed out, "You've got to be able to know when people are blowing smoke at you."

Skills and Problems: Fundamentally Interconnected

It has been argued in the literature that project managers require certain skills in order to be effective. It has also been argued that project managers need to be able to handle certain problems in order to be effective. The results of this study suggest that these two perspectives are not contradictory but are fundamentally compatible. When the set of required skills is considered side by side with the set of critical problems project managers face, the complementary nature of these two perspectives is evident. This is illustrated in Table 3.

Without arguing which comes first, it is clear that either (a) project managers require certain skills in order to deal effectively with the factors most likely to create problems for them in managing the project, or, (b) because certain problems are most likely to confront project managers, they require particular skills in order to handle them.

While this one-on-one matching in Table 3 obviously oversimplifies the dynamic nature of project management, it does have an inherent logical appeal. Since communication breakdowns are likely to create project management

14

Skills–Problems Interconnected in Project Management	
Communication	Breakdowns in Communication
Organizational	Insufficient Planning
	Resources Inadequate
Team Building	Team Members Uncommitted
	Weak Inter-Unit Integration
Leadership	Unclear Goals/Direction
	Interpersonal Conflicts
Coping	Handling Changes
Technological	Meeting ("Unrealistic") Deadlines

Table 3

problems, effective project managers need to cultivate their communications (persuading and listening) skills. Project managers with good organizational skills are likely to be more effective at planning and subsequently allocating resources. Unless project managers are able to build a strong project team, they are likely to be plagued by problems caused by poorly committed team members and interdepartmental conflict. Project goals are likely to be more easily understood when the project manager's leadership is consistent. Interpersonal conflicts will likely diminish when project managers set clear standards of performance and demonstrate their trust in, and respect for, others. The inevitable changes, which accompany any project, will be less problematic when not only coped with calmly but also when handled with flexibility and creativity. Finally, problems created when deadlines and schedules are unrealistic may be minimized through a project manager's problem-finding ability and experience in getting things back on track.

What was found underscores the claim that the primary problems of project managers are not technical but human. Improving project managers' technological capabilities will be helpful only to the extent that this improves their abilities to communicate, be organized, build teams, provide leadership, and deal comfortably with change. The challenge for technical managers, or for those moving from technical into managerial positions, is to recognize the need for, and to develop where necessary, interpersonal skills.

References

1. Archibald, R. 1975. *Managing High-Technology Programs and Projects.* New York: John Wiley and Sons.

Kerzner, H. 1982. *Project Management for Executives.* New York: Van Nostrand Reinold.

Stuckenbruck, L. 1976. Ten Attributes of the Proficient Project Manager. *Proceedings of the Project Management Institute.* Montreal: 40–47.

Thamhain, H., and D. Wilemon. 1978. Skill Requirements of Engineering Project Managers. *Twenty-Sixth IEEE Joint Engineering Management Conference.*

2. Romans, D.D. 1986. *Managing Projects: A Systems Perspective.* New York: Elsevier Science Publishing.

3. Badaway, M. 1982. *Developing Managerial Skills in Scientists and Engineers.* New York: Van Nostrand Reinold.

4. Hitchcock, B. 1967. Problems of First-Line Supervisors. *Research Management* 10, no. 6: 385–397.

Selecting Project Managers: An Integrated List of Predictors

Dr. Normand Pettersen, Université du Québec à Trois-Rivières, Québec, Canada

Project Management Journal 22, no. 2 (June 1991)

A S AN ORGANIZATIONAL FORM, project management is both flexible and changing and appears to provide a promising answer to the challenge of modern organizational complexity. However, this form of management, more organic than functional, has its less advantageous point too. It seems to be accepted in the field that project managers who evolve within a context made more difficult by the variety and complexity of its activities—a context characterized by disorder, ambiguity, and disjunction between formal authority and responsibility—need to develop skills different from those of their colleagues in functional management. Consequently, it becomes extremely important for the organization to take these particular requirements into account when selecting a manager who will be able to bring his projects to a successful conclusion.

A number of articles and other publications in the last fifteen years have discussed the particular characteristics of project management and its consequent demands. However, this literature is a result of isolated efforts and fragmented contributions, and it is therefore difficult for readers to distinguish recurring factors or common points that would help them put together a profile of the ideal project manager—if such a profile exists.

The aim of this article is to provide an integrated requirements profile specifically designed for selecting project managers. The profile is, to the extent possible, based on existing literature. The term "integrated" is used to show that the proposed list of specifications will be based on a coherent model of efficient performance at work, instead of simply presenting a "grocery list" of requirements, as is often the case. As far as a profile designed specifically for selection purposes is concerned, this means that the requirements and predictors included in it will be defined in terms of skills, aptitudes, and personal characteristics being transpositions directed toward job requirements. Finally, the profile will attempt to integrate the most significant publications in the field of performance

17

predictors for project managers in order to take advantage of knowledge and experience already gained.

A Profile for Selection Purposes

The profile, or list of specifications, presented here was developed in two major stages. It was first necessary to bring together all information published to date on project management. A review of the literature was carried out, concentrating mainly on North American texts. Sixty or so specialized publications were analyzed and then summarized around two main themes: first, the functions, tasks, and roles of a project manager, and second, the demands of the work in terms of training, experience, aptitudes, abilities, skills, and other personal characteristics. This review (33) (34) formed the basis of the second stage, which was to draw up a list of specifications suitable for use in the selection process. A basic framework was required to structure the mass of gathered information into a coherent model. The method used for this delicate analysis and synthesis task was inspired by similar work in the field of general management, such as the Academy of Management and Development Dimensions International's American Association of Collegiate Schools of Business Outcome Measurement Project (2), the American Management Association and McBer & Company's Competency Program (7), Gerstein Reisman and Associates' Selection Profile (19), and other contributions (6) (8) (20) (21) (23) (27).

The list thus obtained is presented in tabular form in Table 1. It proposes twenty-one predictors grouped into five sets. Each predictor is conceptually defined by the main dimensions found in the literature. For practical purposes, however, these predictors should be tailored to each individual case by means of indicators specific to the position to be filled and according to the selection tools chosen. These predictors have been defined in task-related terms specially to be used with content-validated selection tools, for example, interviews, simulations like the in-basket (29), group discussions, and other assessment center methodology techniques (46).

The first set, "Problem Solving," is a logical result of three predictors, ranging from problem analysis to decision-making. The predictor, "Problem Analysis," deals with a person's ability to handle information; it is the most closely related to her mental and intellectual potential. The predictor, "Judgment and Practical Sense," based largely on the candidate's experience, refers to the actual content of the solutions or decisions proposed. Finally, "Decisiveness" represents the tendency to make decisions or apply solutions, regardless of their quality.

The second set, "Administration," brings together what are usually known as management skills ("Planning and Organization" and "Control"), political aspects ("Strategy and Organizational Know-How"), and technical aspects ("Specialized Knowledge") of management.

The third set contains the main predictors relating to "Supervision and Project Team Management." The first four predictors are concerned with the manager's behavior toward individual team members, and the other two, with management of the team as a whole.

The fourth set is composed of basic general skills in "Interpersonal Relations."

The last set, "Other Personal Qualities," lumps together various other personal characteristics.

This profile for selection purpose is based on a model of performance at work that can be represented by the following formula:

Performance = Abilities × Motivation × Personality

Without going into the subtleties of industrial organizational psychology, individual determinants of performance at work can be classified according to three variables: abilities, motivation, and personality (15). Abilities include cognitive capabilities, such as skills and knowledge; in other words, what a person knows and can do. Abilities are the result of aptitudes that are developed through time by all forms of learning and experience. The profile proposed here contains several predictors belonging to this category, which includes the four predictors making up the "Administration" set (nos. 4 to 7) and the six in "Supervision and Project Team Management" (nos. 8 to 13), as well as the predictors "Problem Analysis" (no. 1), "Judgment and Practical Sense" (no. 2), "Oral Communication" (no. 14) and "Interpersonal Influence, Persuasion, and Negotiation" (no. 15).

While abilities relate to what an individual **is able** to do, motivation concerns rather what that person **wants** to do. In other words, from the employer's point of view, motivation is shown by the candidate's will to use the abilities he has for the benefit of the organization and its objectives. Motivation explains the efforts and direction applied by an individual as exhibited in behavior. This category brings together evaluative variables such as needs, values, and interests. The list contains three such predictors: "Ascendancy" (no. 16), "Need to Achieve and Proactivity" (no. 17), and "Interest in the Job" (no. 21).

Personality may be defined by a set of affective traits, which are propensities to react in a certain way to a given situation or stimulus (14) (36). In a way, the personality gives the style to behavior triggered by the motivation variables. The list contains three personality predictors: "Self Confidence, Maturity, and Emotional Stability" (no. 18), "Loyalty, Honesty, and Integrity (no. 19), and "Tolerance toward Ambiguity and Openness to Change" (no. 20). As far as "Decisiveness" (no. 3) is concerned, it could be classified either in this category or in the motivation category. From a practitioner's point of view, the category into which a particular variable is placed is not determining; what matters is the overall capacity of the model to predict the future performance of project managers. There are more examples of predictors that could be classified in other categories. Clearly, nos. 8, 10, 11, 12, or even 5, are not purely "abilities"; all have an affective component, also.

Thus, the model described above is a tool to ensure that the three major categories explaining performance at work (abilities, motivation, and personality) are present in the profile to be used so that selection is based on the most significant variables. Inspired by Maier (30), the model indicates also that performance depends on the multiplication of the categories of variables. For example, a highly competent candidate who is not motivated will not perform adequately, nor will a highly motivated candidate who lacks competence. In the same way, a competent and motivated candidate whose personality prevents him from integrating harmoniously into his working environment will have considerable difficulty in producing a satisfactory output.

Screening Specifications

Before the selection process itself, a preliminary sifting of candidates, known as screening, is usually done. Screening is based, above all, on the candidate's education and experience, normally using information contained in the curriculum vitae, application form, or employment dossier. The following paragraphs outline what experts have to say on the subject.

Basic Academic Training

First, the project manager ideally should hold a university degree (3) (25) (28) (44). This basic education may be either in the field of engineering or another related technical discipline relevant to the project (10), or in the field of management, or preferably both (11) (13) (32) (38). It should be noted that a university degree, while not the only way, is certainly one of the best ways to acquire such technical and cognitive predictors.

Some experts believe that management education should prevail over technical education (5), while others are less categorical, saying that the balance should vary according to the nature and size of the project (17) (40). For example, a small project involving a single discipline will require technical skills above all, while a large multidisciplinary project will oblige the manager to spend more time on management activities. The project manager can, in fact, delegate the technical aspects and concentrate on managing the project that should always remain a primary responsibility. However, to be competent in a particular field, and to have previous achievements, can have a quite positive impact in establishing credibility with technical experts. In a world of specialists, it is considered suspect for a manager to be only a generalist (13) (39).

List of Predictors for Project Managers

A. Problem Solving (17)

1. Problem Analysis (39) (45)

Mental and conceptual abilities
Ability to deal quickly with large quantities of information
Identify significant problems
Look beyond symptoms to find the cause
Gather and analyze data that are essential to make a diagnosis
Develop all possible solutions and their consequences

2. Judgment and Practical Sense (10) (39) (40) (43) (45)

Choose wisely among possible solutions
Make decisions and apply solutions that take into account the constraints of the project and its environment
Always bear in mind the overall perspective of the project and not just one of its facets; concentrate on the problem as a whole

3. Decisiveness (4) (10) (13) (31) (43) (45)

Propensity to make decisions
Committed to decisions, even in difficult or delicate situations where the consequences could be personally unpleasant
Set up a concrete strategy for implementing the decision (action planning, delegating responsibilities, fixing objectives, follow-up mechanisms and assessing results)

B. Administration

4. Planning and Organization (1) (4) (10) (12) (13) (26) (31) (38) (39) (45)

Identify objectives and priorities
Establish work timetables
Organize resources to achieve the objectives
Define tasks and work methods

5. Control (1) (4) (10) (12) (18) (32) (43) (45)

Maintain everyday activities in line with objectives and project deadlines
Ensure follow-up and make corrections if necessary
Follow budgets and exercise financial control

6. Strategy and Organizational Know-How (10) (13) (31) (39)

Take steps to be well informed
Build formal and informal collaboration networks
Know who to talk to outside the team or service when necessary
Know the organization and its operation
Ability to work in harmony with the organization's political reality
Ability to implicate others to reach objectives

Table 1 (con't on next page)

7. **Specialized Knowledge** (10) (13) (25) (31) (39) (40) (43)

   Know the information, principles, theories, and techniques that are useful for the various tasks to be done

   This knowledge can be related to management (planning and control tools, accounting, finance, contracts, decision-making tools, behavioral sciences, and so on), the technology to be used, the product or service offered, the market, production, or marketing

C. Supervision and Project Team Management

8. **Delegation of Responsibilities** (4) (41) (45)

   Believe fundamentally in others

   Structure clearly the tasks to be carried out, while leaving enough latitude for initiative on the part of team members

   Delegate responsibility to the appropriate level

   Share part of the responsibility with team members

   Allocate authority and resources to team members to enable them to make significant decisions in their fields of responsibility and competence

   Ability to work with subordinates who are clearly identified as experts in their fields without being either too direct or too deferential

9. **Team Structuring**

   Structure tasks to be carried out and communicate them clearly (see no. 4, Planning and Organization)

   Ability to use power unilaterally

   Use reinforcement to stimulate team members

   Establish control mechanisms that favor task accomplishment according to objectives and correct them if necessary (see no. 5, Control)

10. **Consideration toward Team Members**

    Behave kindly toward team members

    Identify their needs and ensure their satisfaction

    Fair

11. **Development of Team Members**

    Frequently assess the performance of each team member and give him feedback

    Identify training needs of team members on the basis of their present and future tasks

    Set up training strategies and ensure they are carried out

    Demonstrate the importance of training by devoting financial and human resources and personal time to it

12. **Teamwork, Flexibility, and Cooperation** (19) (39) (40) (45)

    Ability to work as part of a group

    Recognize the circumstances that require teamwork or a team decision

    Maintain a climate that encourages the participation and implication of each team member

    Receptive toward other people's points of view

    Prepared to change own opinion and compromise

Table 1 (con't)

13. Resolving Conflicts (4) (10) (26) (38)

Ability to coordinate specialists from different fields
Recognize a conflicting situation and resolve it efficiently (see A, Problem Solving)
Know conflict psychology

D. Interpersonal Relations

14. Oral Communication (4) (10) (19) (39) (40) (43) (45)

Communicate efficiently in exchanges with others
Make efficient verbal presentations
Concretize communications in respect to the project

15. Interpersonal Influence, Persuasion, and Negotiation (39) (45)

Aware of the feelings, needs, and expectations of others
Conscious of the effect of one's behavior on others
Ability to influence others toward realizing objectives
Bring interlocutor around to own point of view while maintaining a good relationship

16. Ascendancy

Liking for command
Need to dominate others and not be dominated
Concerned by one's influence on others

E. Other Personal Qualities

17. Need to Achieve and Proactivity (31) (43) (45)

Need to excel, to achieve something unique
Constant desire to do better, to be the best
Directed toward action and results
Dynamism, relentlessness, energy
Optimism, belief in ability to influence events around oneself

18. Self Confidence, Maturity, and Emotional Stability (10) (13) (43) (45)

Confidence in self and abilities
Ready to live with personal consequences of difficult decisions (see No. 3,
    Decisiveness)
Emotionally stable and strong
Able to control emotions
Short- and long-term resistance to stress

19. Loyalty, Honesty, and Integrity (31) (39)

Endorse the organization's politics and values
Place the organization's interests before own
Respect superiors
Respect engagements
Professional and personal integrity

Table 1 (con't)

20. Tolerance toward Ambiguity and Openness to Change (10) (13) (19) (31) (43) (45)

Accept uncertainty and unforeseen circumstances that are inevitable during a project

Desire to work among more supple organizational structures such as matrical structure or its variants

Propensity to change plans, approaches, strategies, policies, or practices according to the demands of the situation

21. Interest in the Job

Intrinsic motivation for the work itself and its different activities

Hopes and career plan that correspond to the opportunities offered

Interest in the working conditions (place, timetable, salary, and so on)

Table 1 (con't)

Practical Experience and On-the-Job Training

Experience and on-the-job training are of vital importance in project management (18) and should preferably be acquired progressively by carrying out different functions at different levels (22) (42). It is good for the candidate to have worked for an experienced professional able to pass on the practical knowledge needed for a variety of assignments (9).

Several years of diversified experience in the field seem essential for two main reasons. First, the ability to visualize the project as a whole in all its technical, social, and political complexity is a skill that cannot be obtained in a few weeks, no matter how varied the work. Second, the interdisciplinary approach fundamental in project management also requires time to develop in project managers who have, for the most part, specialized in a particular discipline very early in their training (42).

Remarks

The profile described in this article presents two important advantages. First, the predictors have been integrated into a simple model, which is nevertheless based on rigorous psychological foundations, to form a diagnostic tool that promotes better understanding of the individual determinants of performance at work (see (35) for a more complete model). Second, it is strengthened by the knowledge and experience of many experts in the field, since a large body of project management literature has been taken into account in formulating it.

To benefit fully from the profile, a decision-maker needs to know its limits. First, the list of predictors is by no means exhaustive. Only those predictors that can be applied to a wide range of project management positions were included. For example, an organization wishing to recruit a project manager to work in a developing country would need to add other specifications.

Second, the predictors are interdependent to a certain extent. As is the case with all typologies based on psychological characteristics, it is almost impossible to obtain dimensions that are completely unrelated. For example, how could a candidate have sound judgment and good practical sense (no. 2) without also having a minimum of problem analysis skills (no. 1)? It is also clear that interpersonal influence and persuasion (no. 15) could help resolve conflicts (no. 13). This problem, however, is not serious because a slight overlapping between dimensions does not undermine the validity of the list's content, nor does it interfere significantly with its practical worth.

Finally, the predictors are not weighted according to certain task-related parameters. Spitz (39), for example, observes that the importance of skills and areas of expertise varies in conformity with the stage of the project. Katz and Kahn (24), for their part, consider that the skills mix should fluctuate in relation to the manager's position in the hierarchy. It would thus be extremely important to weight the predictors, as Posner (37) did, but possibly following Davis' (12) excellent classification of various kinds of project management practices. Unfortunately, the present state of the research does not yet allow such refinements to be made.

Acknowledgment: The author wishes to thank professor Rene Garneau for his helpful comments on an earlier draft of this paper and translator Christine Gardner for her editing assistance.

References

1. Adams, J.R., and S.E. Barndt. 1978. Organizational Life Cycle Implication for Major Projects. *Project Management Quarterly* 9, no. 4: 32–39.

2. Albanese, R. 1987. Outcome Measurement and Management Education. *The Academy of Management Newsletter* 17, no. 2: 12–15.

3. Allen, R.D. 1980. Project Management Challenges in the 1980s. *Project Management Quarterly* 11, no. 4: 19–23.

4. Andersson, M. 1984. Improving Project Management Capabilities. *C.A. Magazine* 117, no. 10: 86–90.

5. Assad, M.G., and G.P.J. Pelser. 1983. Project Management: A Goal-Directed Approach. *Project Management Quarterly* 14, no. 1: 49–58.

6. Bennis, W., and B. Namus. 1985. *Leaders.* New York: Harper & Row.

7. Boyatzis, R.E. 1982. *The Competent Manager.* New York: John Wiley.

8. Campbell, J.P., M.D. Dunnette, E.E. Lawler III, and K.E. Weick. 1970. *Managerial Behavior, Performance, and Effectiveness.* New York: McGraw–Hill.

9. Cole, V.E., W.B. Ball, and D.S. Barrie. 1978. Managing the Project. *Project Management Quarterly* 9, no. 1: 34–49.

10. Conseil du tresor du Canada. 1979. *Manuel de la politique administrative, Chapitre 141, Chefs de grands projets.* Ottawa: Gouvernement du Canada.

11. Cook, D.L., and J. Granger. 1975. How Well Educated Is Your Prospective Project Manager? *Project Management Quarterly* 6, no. 2: 26–28.

12. Davis, K. 1969. The Role of Project Management in Scientific Manufacturing. In *Systems, Organizations, Analysis, Management: A Book of Readings*, edited by K. Davis, D.I. Cleland, and R. King, 308–314. New York: McGraw-Hill.

13. Declerck, R.P., P. Eymery, and M.A. Crener. 1980. *Le Management strategique des projets*. Paris, France: Editions Hommes et Techniques.

14. Digman, J.M. 1990. Personality Structure: Emergence of the Five-Factor Model. *Annual Review of Psychology* 41: 417–440.

15. Dupont, J.-B. 1987. In *Traite de psychologie du travail*, edited by C. Levy-Leboyer et J.-C. Sperandio, 511–533. Paris: Presses Universitaires de France.

16. Dunnette, M.D. 1976. Aptitudes, Abilities, and Skills. In *Handbook of Industrial and Organizational Psychology*, edited by M.D. Dunnette, 473–520. Chicago, Ill: Rand McNally.

17. Einsiedel, Jr., A.A. 1987. Profile of Effective Project Managers. *Project Management Journal* 18, no. 5: 51–56.

18. Gaddis, P.O. 1959. The Project Manager. *Harvard Business Review* (May–June): 89–97.

19. Gerstein, M., and H. Reisman. 1983. Strategic Selection: Matching Executives to Business Conditions. *Sloan Management Review* 24, no. 2: 33–49.

20. Ghiselli, E.E. 1966. *The Validity of Occupational Aptitude Tests*. New York: John Wiley.

21. ———. 1973. The Validity of Aptitude Tests in Personnel Selection. *Personnel Psychology* 26, no. 2: 461–477.

22. Henderson, D.H. 1972. Career Blueprints for Project Managers. *Project Management Quarterly* 3, no. 3: 11–13.

23. House, R.J., and M.L. Baetz. 1978. Leadership: Some Empirical Generalizations and New Research Directions. Working paper, University of Toronto.

24. Katz, D., and R.L. Kahn. 1978. *The Social Psychology of Organizations*. 2nd ed. rev. New York: John Wiley.

25. Kerzner, H. 1979. Formal Education for Project Management. *Project Management Quarterly* 10, no. 2: 38–44.

26. ———. 1984. *Project Management—A System Approach to Planning, Scheduling and Controlling*. 2nd ed. rev. New York: Van Nostrand Reinhold.

27. Kotter, J.P. 1982. *The General Manager*. New York: Free Press.

28. Leblanc, R.N. 1982. Project Management—Some Future Policy Implications Based on Past Experience. *Optimum* 13, no. 3: 5–19.

29. Lopez, F. 1966. *Evaluating Executive Decision Making: The In-Basket Technique*. New York: American Management Association.

30. Maier, N.R.F. 1973. *Psychology in Industrial Organizations*. 4th ed. rev. Boston: Houghton Mifflin.

31. Martin, C.C. 1976. *Project Management: How to Make it Work*. New York: Amacom.

32. Nina, K., and K. Sasaki. 1983. A New Project Management System Approach: The "Know-How" Based Project Management System. *Project Management Quarterly* 14, no. 1: 65–72.

33. Pettersen, N. 1989a. Description de taches et profil d'exigences du gestionnaire de projet: examen de la documentation nord-americaine. Department d'administration et d'economique, Universite du Quebec a Trois-Rivieres.

34. ———. 1989b. Le gestionnaire de projet. In *La gestion de projet: concepts et pratiques*, edited by M.A. Crener et P. Beaulieu. Montreal: Presse de l'Universite du quebec/Editions Hommes et Techniques (a paraitre).

35. Pettersen, N., and R. Jacob. 1990. Un schema d'integration du comportement de l'individu au travail. VIeme Congres international de l'Association de psychologie de langue francaise, Universite libre de Bruxelles, Nivelles, Belgique.

36. Phares, E.J. 1988. *Introduction to Personality*, 2nd ed. Glenview, Ill: Scott, Foresman Company.

37. Posner, B.Z. 1987. What It Takes to Be a Good Project Manager. *Project Management Journal* 28, no. 1: 51–54.

38. Sharad, D. 1979. Organizing for Project/Construction Management. *Proceedings of the Eleventh Project Management Institute Seminar/Symposium.* Atlanta, Georgia.

39. Spitz, C.J. 1982. The Project Leader: A Study of Task Requirements, Management Skills and Personal Style. Unpublished doctoral dissertation, Case Western Reserve University.

40. Stickney, F.A., and W.R. Johnston. 1980. Communication: The Key to Integration. *Proceedings of the Twelfth Project Management Institute Seminar/Symposium.* Phoenix, Arizona.

41. ———. 1983. Delegation and Sharing of Authority by the Project Manager. *Project Management Quarterly* 14, no. 1: 42–63.

42. Stuckenbruck, L.C. 1976a. The Effective Project Manager. *Project Management Quarterly* 7, no. 1: 26–27.

43. ———. 1976b. The Ten Attributes of the Proficient Project Manager. *Proceedings of the Eighth Project Management Institute Seminar/Symposium.* Montreal, Canada.

44. ———. 1977. The Educational Path to Project Management. *Proceedings of the Ninth Project Management Institute Seminar/Symposium.* Chicago, Illinois.

45. Thornberry, N.E., and J.R. Weintraub. 1983. The Project Manager: What It Takes to Be a Good One. *Project Management Quarterly* 14, no. 1: 73–76.

46. Thornton III, G.C., and W.C. Byham. 1982. *Assessment Centers and Managerial Performance.* New York: Academic Press.

Project Leadership: Understanding and Consciously Choosing Your Style

Dennis P. Slevin, The Joseph M. Katz Graduate School of Business,
University of Pittsburgh
Jeffrey K. Pinto, College of Business Administration, University of Maine

Project Management Journal 22, no. 1 (March 1991)

T RYING TO HELP PROJECT MANAGERS become better leaders has always been a difficult task. Project managers must rely on a variety of skills in order to successfully manage their projects. Not the least of these required skills is the ability to motivate, inspire, and lead the project team. True leadership on the part of the project manager has been shown time and again to be one of the most important single characteristics in successfully implementing projects (1) (2) (3). As a result, the more one is able to understand this complex concept, the better able one will be to manage projects and train future project managers in the tasks and skills required for their jobs.

Leadership is a complex process that is crucial to successful project management. The principal difficulty with studying leadership is that we know at once so much and so little about the concept. Behavioral scientists have been studying the leadership problem over the past half-century in an attempt to better understand the process and to come up with prescriptive recommendations concerning effective leadership behaviors. Years of careful research have generated a variety of findings that at best are sometimes confusing to the practicing manager and, at worst, are often internally inconsistent. For example, the following eleven propositions have all been suggested to guide leader behavior:

- Leaders will be most effective when they show a high level of concern for both the task and the employees (their subordinates) (4).
- Leaders should be task-oriented under conditions when they have either high or low control over the group. When they only have moderate control over the group, leaders should be people-oriented (5).

29

- To be effective, leaders must base their decision-making styles on how important employee acceptance of the decision will be. They should seek participation by subordinates in decision-making accordingly (6).
- Leaders will be accepted and will motivate employees to the extent that their behavior helps employees progress toward valued goals and provides guidance or clarification not already present in the work situation (7).
- A participative approach to leadership will lead to improved employee morale and increase commitment to the organization (8).
- Under stressful conditions (e.g., time pressure), an autocratic leadership style will lead to greater productivity (9). A minimum level of friendliness or warmth will enhance this effect (10).
- Even when a leader has all the needed information to make a decision, and the problem is clearly structured, employees prefer a participative approach to decision-making (11).
- Effective leaders tend to exhibit high levels of intelligence, initiative, personal needs for occupational achievement, and self-confidence (12, 13).
- Effective leadership behavior can depend on the organizational setting; therefore, similar behaviors may have different consequences in different settings (14, 15).
- Leadership behavior may not be important if subordinates are skilled, if tasks are structured or routine, if technology dictates the required actions, and if the administrative climate is supportive and fair (16).
- Leadership behavior can be divided into task behavior (one-way communication) and relationship behavior (two-way communication). An effective leadership style using these behaviors can be selected according to the maturity level of subordinates relative to accomplishing the task (17).

This list of principles of leadership and leader behavior presents a bewildering set of premises for project managers. In some cases, these points seem to actively disagree with each other. For example, some researchers say that a participatory leadership style is best for all situations, while other work suggests that a participatory style is more effective in some situations, and with some types of subordinates, than in others. Some of the conclusions argue that specific character traits of the leader determine effectiveness while other work states that it is, in fact, the dynamics of the interaction of the leader with subordinates that determines effectiveness. Finally, other authors have concluded that, under some conditions, leadership style is not important at all.

So where does this leave the project manager? These research results certainly reinforce the perception that the process of project leadership is confusing, complex, and often contradictory. What would help the practicing project manager is a day-to-day "working" model that clarifies some aspects of the concept of leadership, suggests alternative leadership styles that may be used, and provides some practical recommendations on conditions under which alternative leadership styles might be used. The purpose of this article is to describe a *cognitive* approach to leadership that will help the project manager consciously select the leadership style correct for alternative situations.

Critical Dimensions of Information and Decision Authority

Suppose that you are a leader of a five-person project team. You are faced with a problem that is complex, yet a decision must be made. From the standpoint of leadership, before you make the decision, you must answer two "pre-decisional" questions:

1. Where do you get the information input? (Whom do you ask for relevant information?)

2. Where should you place the decision authority for this problem? (Who makes the decision?)

The first question asks which members of the group you head will furnish information about a particular decision. The second asks to what extent you maintain all the decision authority and make the decision yourself, or to what extent you "share" your decision authority with members of your project team and have them make the decision with you in a more or less democratic fashion.

The first dimension is one of information; the second is one of decision authority. These two critical dimensions are essential for effective leadership, and they have been plotted on the graph in Figure 1, The Bonoma/Slevin Leadership Model. As a leader, you may request large amounts of subordinate information input into a decision or very small amounts. This is the vertical axis-information input. Secondly, as a leader, your decision-making style may range all the way from making the decision entirely yourself to sharing power with the group and having the final decision made entirely as a group decision. This is the horizontal axis-decision authority.

By using percentile scores, any leadership style may be plotted in the two-dimensional space. For convenience, we will refer to the horizontal axis (decision authority) first and the vertical axis (information) second in discussing scores.

Four Leadership Styles

Using the plotting system, we can describe almost every leadership style (refer to Figure 1). The four extremes of leaders you have known (depicted in the four corners of the grid) are as follows:

Autocrat (100, 0). Such managers solicit little or no information from their project teams and make managerial decisions solely by themselves.

Consultative Autocrat (100, 100). In this managerial style, intensive information input is elicited from the members, but such formal leaders keep all substantive decision-making authority to themselves.

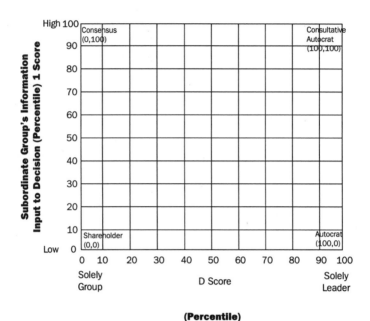

Figure 1 The Bonoma/Slevin Leadership Model

Consensus Manager (0, 100). Purely consensual managers throw open the problem to the group for discussion (information input) and simultaneously allow or encourage the entire group to make the relevant decision.

Shareholder Manager (0, 0). This position is literally poor management. Little or no information input and exchange takes place within the group context, while the group itself is provided ultimate authority for the final decision.

The advantages of the leadership model, apart from its practical simplicity, become more apparent when we consider three traditional aspects of leadership and managerial decision style:

- Participative management
- Delegation
- Personal and organizational pressures affecting leadership.

Participative Management

The concept of "participation" in management is a complex one with different meanings for different individuals. When we discuss the notion of participation with practicing project managers in a consulting setting, the following response is typical: "Oh, I participated with my subordinates on that decision—I asked each of them what they thought before I made the decision."

To the practicing manager, participation is often an informational construct, i.e., permitting sufficient subordinate input to be made before the hierarchical decision is handed down. On the other hand, when we discuss the concept of participation with academics, the following response is typical: "Managers should use participation management more often—they should allow their subordinates to make the final decision with them in a consensual manner."

To the academic, the concept of participation is often an issue of **power**, i.e., moving to the left on the Bonoma/Slevin Model so that decision authority is shared with the group.

In actuality, participation is a **two-dimensional** construct. It involves both the solicitation of information and the sharing of power or decision authority. Neither dimension, in and of itself, is a sufficient indicator of a participative leadership style. Participative management requires equal emphasis on the project manager requesting information and allowing a more democratic decision-making dynamic to be adopted.

Delegation

Good managers delegate effectively. In doing so they negotiate some sort of compromise between the extreme of "abdication"—letting subordinates decide everything—and "autocratic management"—doing everything themselves. We have found the leadership model useful for managers as they delegate work to their subordinates. After exposure to the model, managers are often likely to be more explicit about the informational and decision authority requirements of a delegated task. For example, the project manager might say to his subordinate: "Get the information that you need from my files and also check with Marketing (information). You make the decision yourself (decision authority), but notify me in writing as soon as you have made it so that I am kept informed."

Thus the subordinate understands both the information and decision authority aspects of the delegated tasks. Delegation often fails when the communication is unclear on either or both of these dimensions.

Pressures Affecting Leadership

As a project manager, you may act differently as a leader under different conditions, depending upon three kinds of pressure:
- Problem attributes pressures
- Leader personality pressures
- Organization/group pressures.

Think of the leadership model in terms of a map of the United States. Table 1 summarizes these pressures on leadership style in terms of geographical direction. (For example, a movement "north" is a movement upward on the vertical axis of the leadership model, and so on.)

Problem Attributes

Problem attribute pressures generate eastward forces in the leader. In other words, they often cause leaders to take the majority of or sole decision-making authority on themselves. This is especially true when problems are characterized as:

- Time bound (a quick decision is required)
- Important
- Personal
- Structured and routine.

In such cases, it is very tempting to take "control" over the decisional process personally and "get the job done." However, northward pressures (involving the quest for additional information) can occur as well, given:

- Important decisions
- Decisions in which you as the leader lack the resources to make the decision yourself
- Problems in which subordinate implementation is critical to success.

In these cases, information input and exchange will be maximized. Time pressures tend to push one toward the east, into an "autocratic mode." Implementation concerns push one to the northwest, in search of both more information and the active participation in and support of the decision by subordinates. It is a well-known behavioral finding that people cooperate more in implementing decisions that they have helped make.

Leader Personality

Some managers tend to be inflexible in their leadership style because of who they are and how they like to manage. Our experience has led us to conclude that, in many cases, such managers:

- Have a high need for power
- Are task oriented, or
- Are highly intelligent.

Managers of this type will make many decisions themselves that might otherwise be left to subordinates, and they also may make decisions without acquiring information from the group. People-oriented leaders, on the other hand, will act to maximize information inputs from their subordinates and to share their decision authority as well. Both of these activities are "people processes."

Type of Pressure	Direction of Pressure on Leadership Grid
PROBLEM ATTRIBUTES PRESSURES	
Leader lacks relevant information; problem is ambiguous.	North: more information needed.
Leader lacks enough time to make decision adequately.	South and east: consensus and information collection take time.
Decision is important or critical to leader.	North and east: personal control and information maximized.
Problem is structured or routine.	South and east: little time as possible spent on decision.
Decision implementation by subordinates is critical to success.	West and north: input and consensus required.
LEADER PERSONALITY PRESSURES	
Leader has high need for power.	East: personal control maximized.
Leader is high in need for affiliation, is "people oriented."	North and west: contact with people maximized.
Leader is highly intelligent.	East: personal competence demonstrated.
Leader has high need for achievement.	East: personal contribution maximized.
ORGANIZATIONAL AND GROUP PRESSURES	
Conflict is likely to result from the decision.	North and west: participative aspects of decision-making maximized.
Good leader-group relations exist.	North and west: group contact maximized.
Centrality: formalization of organization is high.	South and east: organization style matched.

Table 1.   Three Leadership Style Pressures

Organizational/Group Pressures

If conflict is likely to result from any decision made, effective managers are most likely to want their subordinates as involved as possible in both the input (northward) and authority (westward) dimensions, so as to help manage the potential conflict. Should good leader/group relations exist, pressure northward (but *not* necessarily westward) will be felt. The leader will feel great pressure to fit into the "culture" of the organization. The research and development lab expects a consensual approach, most business groups expect a consultative autocrat approach, and the factory floor may expect an autocratic approach. It is important to match your style to the norms, needs, and expectations of your subordinates.

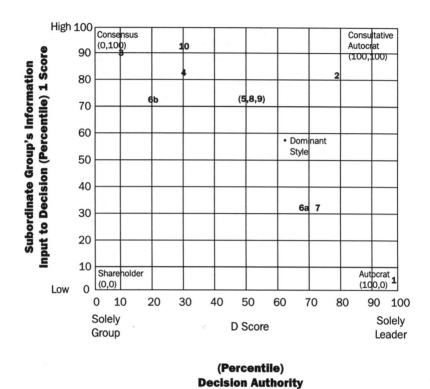

Figure 2   Bonoma/Slevin Leadership Model with Ten Projects Plotted

Flexibility

We argue for a contingency model of leadership. No one style is best for all situations. Rather, the successful manager is flexible and moves around the model as appropriate to the given situation. If time pressures are overwhelming, autocratic decisions may be appropriate. For a majority of management decision-making, the consultative autocrat approach may be the best alternative. And, in dealing with high-tech professionals, engineers, and other specialists, the project manager may choose a more consensual style. The key to success is to **match your leadership style to the situation.**

Examples of the Model in Use

One of the author's executive MBA students, with significant project management responsibility and experience, recently applied the Bonoma/Slevin Model to a number of day-to-day leadership situations he faced. His comments and analysis are shown in Figure 2. These examples clearly show flexibility (the willingness to move around the leadership model on a decision-to-decision basis) and self-insight.

Case Examples for One Project Leader

The following is the analysis of one project manager in a responsible position using the model to analyze ten decisions as described in his own words (18):

> I have elected to analyze the decision process/leadership style I should utilize in ten key projects associated with the assemblage discussed in the introduction.
>
> First, I completed the Jerrell/Slevin Management Instrument. This instrument identified my decision process to be "balanced" in that it is not heavily skewed to any one of the four management styles. The measurement tended to lean toward consultative autocrat.
>
> Second, I asked my superiors as well as my subordinates and peers to categorize my decision/leadership style as autocrat, consultative autocrat, consensus manager, or shareholder manager based on their definitions as previously discussed. Almost unanimously, these individuals categorized my style as consultative autocrat.

Being consciously aware of the above, and the fact that an effective leader must have a leadership style that is flexible to individual situations, I have listed the projects, identified what I feel to be the appropriate leadership style, and estimated the coordinates of this leadership style on the Bonoma/Slevin Leadership Model. They are shown in Table 2.

Findings from Personal Experience

Based on the presentation and discussion of this leadership model with thousands of practicing managers, we would like to share with you some of our conclusions concerning project management and leadership style.

You are more autocratic than you think. In the eyes of your subordinates, you are probably closer to the autocrat on the graph than you are in your own eyes. Why? Because you are the boss, and they are the subordinates. No matter how easygoing, friendly, participative, and supportive you are, you are still the boss. There is almost always a perceived difference in leadership style by the supervisor and subordinates.

But it's O.K. Often when you ask subordinates where they would like their boss to move, they respond, "Things are O.K. as they are." Even though there are perceptual discrepancies concerning leadership style, there may not necessarily be a felt need or pressure for change. The status quo may be O.K.

1. **Project:** Determine if the companies should take cash discounts where economically feasible and ensure these discounts are passed through to the customer.
   Leadership Style: Autocrat (100,0)
   Basis for Leadership Style: The question leads itself to a logical solution (which I am qualified and have the authority to make). Implementation is primarily focused on adequate contacts versus a group consensus/commitment.

2. **Project:** Initiate a study to consider involving the salesmen in overall company profitability.
   a. Should the formula for salesmen's compensation take into consideration the level of gross margin achieved on each sale?
   b. What expenses are controlled by salesmen? How should these expenses be monitored?
   c. Should salesmen be involved in the collection of accounts receivable?
   Leadership Style: Consultative Autocrat (80,80)
   Basis for Leadership Style: Similar to project 1, this question represents a financial control decision to the organization. Implementation of the decision can be performed by focusing on adequate controls and does not require a group consensus. Unlike project 1, I do not feel qualified to autocratically make this decision. It requires a detailed knowledge of current procedures, industry "norms," and individual corporate cultures. Accordingly, considerable consultation and data collection will have to be performed prior to making and implementing a decision.

3. **Project:** Coordinate efforts when a new product is introduced and manufacturer support is not adequate to assure salesmen and service training is appropriate.
   Leadership Style: Consensus Manager (10,90)
   Basis for Leadership Style: The subject is one that requires information from the group as well as a group commitment for successful implementation. The group process will likely generate various alternatives, which will be incorporated into the final decision. Equally important as the leadership style (consensus manager) is the composition of the group. Accordingly, members of management, sales, and several technicians will be asked to participate in this process.

4. **Project:** Investigate combined purchases within zones and throughout the country.
   Leadership Style: Consensus Manager (30,80)
   Basis for Leadership Style: This decision process requires a consensus approach primarily due to the need for group information, support, and implementation. Implementation will require a joint effort of the group with respect to initial purchasing procedures as well as obtaining the manufacturer's approval for combining purchases across regions. Said approval has historically been denied. The probability of such an agreement from the manufacturer is enhanced if approached by a group that has the ability to capitalize on its size and existing relationships.

5. **Project:** Develop and circulate monthly listings of each company's slow-moving inventory.
   Leadership Style: Mix between Consultative Autocrat and Consensus Manager (50,70)
   Basis for Leadership Style: The decision to circulate the lists could be purely autocratic; however, proper implementation will require group acceptance. Therefore, it is important to involve the group. I believe the group will come to the desired outcome. If, however, it becomes apparent that the group does not adequately assess the situation, a shift to a consultative autocrat approach will be implemented due to the underlying importance of this project. (Note: Severity of the problem is exemplified by the existence of inventory days, at certain locations, in excess of 300 days in an industry where inventory days average 65–75 days.)

Table 2. Case Examples for One Project Leader (con't on next page)

6. **Project:** Determine the need for EDP systems coordination, enhancement, and consolidation.
   Leadership Style: Mix between Autocrat and Consensus Manager; 6a (70,30) and 6b (20,70)
   Basis for Leadership Style: This style initially appears contradictory. However, I view this objective as two separate decisions:
   a. How much can be spent (i.e., based on appropriate cost/benefits and risk analysis)?
   b. What systems should be selected and implemented based on financial guidelines?

   Accordingly, I believe the decision in step one (part a) can be made in an autocratic style based on the investor's returns and "value added" requirements, while the actual system and method of implementation can be decided upon as a group consensus.

   The key to the above project is to explain to the project team the critical success factors and parameters existing in Decision 1 and their inherent limitations for Decision 2.

7. **Project:** Develop standardized financial reporting.
   Leadership Style: Autocrat (70,30)
   Basis for Leadership Style: The desired result is a highly structured financial report among each individual organization, which can be utilized for comparison and consolidation purposes. Accordingly, there is virtually no room for flexibility. A limited amount of consulting may be performed to enhance the investor's understanding of the industry. It is highly unlikely that this will have an impact on the report structure. (It is important to note that additional information applicable to the industry may be supplementally obtained, but the primary report will be consolidated and compared with other investments. Hence, flexibility is severely limited.)

8. **Project:** Coordinate efforts to reduce parts inventory.
   Leadership Style: Mix between Consultative Autocrat and Consensus Manager (50,70)
   Basis for Leadership Style: Similar to project 5. A consultative autocrat approach may be necessary to stress the point that something must be done. Yet, a consensus manager approach is necessary to obtain information, utilize the appropriate expertise, and ensure implementation.

9. **Project:** Develop a joint program to dispose of used equipment.
   Leadership Style: Mix between Consultative Autocrat and Consensus Manager (50,70)
   Basis for Leadership Style: This project is designed to dovetail on project 5. I believe the same leadership style is appropriate.

10. **Project:** Determine the feasibility and cost benefits of joint advertising and telemarketing.
    Leadership Style: Consensus Manager (30,90)
    Basis for Leadership Style: Implementation of this project requires group commitment. If the group decides that joint advertising and telemarketing are beneficial, then considerable planning and coordination will be necessary for project success.

Table 2. Case Examples for One Project Leader (con't)

It is easy to move north and south. It is easy to move vertically on the graph. Why? Because management is a job of communication. It is easy to collect more information or less information before you make the decision. The information dimension is the least resistant to change.

It is hard to move west. Most managers, in our experience, find it quite threatening to move westward too quickly. This hesitation is because a westward

Scoring Instructions

1. Record your D score (the sum of the answers to items 1–10).

   D = _____

2. Record your I score (the sum of the answers to items 11–20).

   I = _____

3. Determine your percentile score from the table below.

D			I	
Raw Score	Percentile		Raw Score	Percentile
19	1		22	1
20	1		23	1
21	1		24	1
22	3		25	2
23	5		26	2
24	6		27	4
25	9		28	6
26	12		29	7
27	15		30	8
28	22		31	15
29	27		32	18
30	37		33	26
31	42		34	39
32	53		35	48
33	64		36	56
34	72		37	69
35	81		38	78
36	85		39	84
37	91		40	87
38	94		41	92
39	97		42	96
40	98		43	98
41	99		44	99
42	99		45	99
43	100		46	100

4. Plot yourself on the grid.

Percentiles are estimates based on data collected from 191 American managers.

Figure 3. Jerrell/Slevin Management Instrument

movement upsets the basic power realities in the organization. If your head is in the noose, and if things do not work out, then it is hard to turn the decisions over to your subordinates.

If subordinates' expectations are not met, morale can suffer. What would happen if your subordinates expected you to use a (50, 90) process and instead you made the decision using a (90, 10) style? That's right, dissatisfaction and morale problems result. As mentioned before, decision process can be as important as decision outcome, especially from the standpoint of motivating subordinates.

Be flexible. A successful manager is autocratic when he needs to be, consultative when necessary, and consensual when the situation calls for it. He moves around the leadership space to fit the needs of the situation. Unsuccessful man-

JERRELL/SLEVIN MANAGEMENT INSTRUMENT

Circle the number for each item that represents your best estimate.

	STRONGLY DISAGREE	DISAGREE	NEUTRAL	AGREE	STRONGLY AGREE
1. I don't like it when others disagree with me.	1	2	3	4	5
2. I like quick results.	1	2	3	4	5
3. I find it hard to accept others' decisions.	1	2	3	4	5
4. I have a strong ego.	1	2	3	4	5
5. Once I make up my mind, I stick to it.	1	2	3	4	5
6. I enjoy giving orders.	1	2	3	4	5
7. The work group should determine its own vacation schedule.	5	4	3	2	1
8. The work group should determine its own work schedule.	5	4	3	2	1
9. I feel comfortable being placed in a powerful position.	1	2	3	4	5
10. I like working in a group situation.	5	4	3	2	1
TOTAL D SCORE (Items 1–10 above)	**D =** _____				

	STRONGLY DISAGREE	DISAGREE	NEUTRAL	AGREE	STRONGLY AGREE
11. It is easier to make a decision in a group.	1	2	3	4	5
12. Groups usually take up more time than they are worth.	5	4	3	2	1
13. I often ask for information from subordinates.	1	2	3	4	5
14. Groups give a deeper analysis of a problem.	1	2	3	4	5
15. I often use what subordinates have to say.	1	2	3	4	5
16. No one else can know as much about the problem as I do.	5	4	3	2	1
17. I usually make my decision before calling a staff meeting.	5	4	3	2	1
18. Better decisions are made in group situations.	1	2	3	4	5
19. A group is no better than its best member.	5	4	3	2	1
20. Group decisions are the best.	1	2	3	4	5
TOTAL I SCORE (Items 11–20 above)	**I =** _____				

agers are inflexible and try the same style in all situations. Most managers feel that their scores on the Jerrell/Slevin Management Instrument is a function of the particular jobs they have been in over the last few months. Be flexible and match your leadership style to the job.

Overview: Implications for Your Leadership Style

The leadership framework presented in our model forces the manager to ask two key questions concerning decision making:
- Whom do I ask?
- Who makes the decision?

Obtaining accurate information input from one's subordinate group is crucial to effective project management. Similarly, decision-making authority must be located in the right place vis-a-vis the leader's group.

The model presented here might be more broadly applied to projects in general. Successful projects are implemented through sufficient access to and judicious use of both information and power. At the start of any project one might be well advised to review the status of project information and power. Consider the following questions:

- Where will the project information come from?
- Does the project team have adequate access to information...
  - From top management
  - From peers
  - From technical experts
  - From government regulators
  - From the formal MIS
  - From other team members?
- Who has the power to make decisions and get those decisions implemented?

Once the team has developed technical/analytical solutions, who has the organizational authority to get action? Do the project leaders have the decision authority they need to command resources, people, material, and behavior change? If some project leaders do not have formal power, as can sometimes be the case, do they have access to top management or other organizational sources of power?

In summary, successful project management is greatly affected by the information and power in the system. Successful project managers have always had an intuitive sense for these issues. This model is an attempt to provide the project manager with a framework that can be used in a conscious and analytical way to enhance project success.

Acknowledgment: The authors are indebted to Thomas V. Bonoma for the development of the Bonoma/Slevin Leadership Model and to S. Lee Jerrell for the development of the Jerrell/Slevin Management Instrument

Notes: Portions of this article were adapted from the chapter on leadership in *The Whole Manager: How to Increase Your Professional and Personal Effectiveness*, by Dennis P. Slevin, New York: AMACOM, 1989, (c) 1989 by Dennis P. Slevin. Used with permission. And Leadership, Motivation and the Project Manager, by Dennis P. Slevin and Jeffrey K. Pinto in *The Project Management Handbook*, D.I. Cleland and W.R. King (Eds.), New York: Van Nostrand Reinhold Co., 1988.

References

1. Slevin, D.P., and J.K. Pinto. 1988. Leadership, Motivation, and the Project Manager. In *The Project Management Handbook*, 2nd ed., edited by D.I. Cleland and W.R. King, 739–770. New York: Van Nostrand Reinhold Co.

2. Baker, B.N., D.C. Murphy, and D. Fisher. 1983. Factors Affecting Project Success. In *The Project Management Handbook*, edited by D.I. Cleland and W.R. King, 69–85. New York: Van Nostrand Reinhold Co.

3. Posner, B.Z. 1987. What It Takes to Be a Good Project Manager. *Project Management Journal* 28, no. 1: 51–54.

4. Blake, R.R., and J. Mouton. 1964. *The Managerial Grid.* Houston, TX: Gulf Publishing.

5. Fiedler, F.E. 1978. Contingency Models and the Leadership Process. In *Advances in Experimental Social Psychology*, edited by L. Berkowitz, vol. 11. New York: Academic Press.

6. Vroom, V.H., and P.W. Yetton. 1973. *Leadership and Decision Making.* Pittsburgh, PA: University of Pittsburgh Press.

7. House, R.J. 1971. A Path-Goal Theory of Leadership Effectiveness. *Administrative Science Quarterly* 16: 321–333.

8. Fleishman, E.A. 1973. Twenty Years of Consideration and Structure. In *Current Developments in the Study of Leadership*, edited by E.A. Fleishman and J.G. Hunt. Carbondale, IL: Southern Illinois University Press.

9. Fodor, E.M. 1976. Group Stress, Authoritarian Style of Control, and Use of Power. *Journal of Applied Psychology* 61: 313–318.

10. Tjosvold, D. 1984. Effects of Leader Warmth and Directiveness on Subordinate Performance on a Subsequent Task. *Journal of Applied Psychology* 69: 422–427.

11. Heilman, M.E., H.A. Hornstein, J.H. Cage, and J.K. Herschlag. 1984. Reactions to Prescribed Leader Behavior as a Function of Role Perspective: The Case of the Vroom-Yetton Model. *Journal of Applied Psychology* 69: 50–60.

12. Stodgdill, R. 1984. *Handbook of Leadership.* New York: Free Press.

13. Ghiselli, E. 1971. *Exploration of Managerial Talent.* Santa Monica, CA: Goodyear.

14. Dansereau, F., G. Graen, and B. Haga. 1975. A Vertical Dyad Linkage Approach to Leadership Within Formal Organizations: A Longitudinal Investigation of Role Making Process. *Organizational Behavior and Human Performance* 13: 45–78.

15. Salancik, G.R., B.J. Calder, K.M. Rowland, H. Leblibici, and M. Conway. 1975. Leadership as an Outcome of Social Structure and Process: A Multi-Dimensional Analysis. In *Leadership Frontiers*, edited by J.G. Hunt and L.L. Larson. Kent, OH: Kent State University Press.

16. Kerr, S., and J.M. Jermier. 1978. Substitutes for Leadership: Their Meaning and Measurement. *Organizational Behavior and Human Performance* 22, 375–403.

17. Hersey, P., and K.H. Blanchard. 1977. *Management of Organizational Behavior: Utilizing Human Resources.* 3rd ed. Englewood Cliffs, NJ: Prentice-Hall.

18. Sprecher, W.E. 1987. Private Communication (April).

Developing Project Management Skills

Hans J. Thamhain, Bentley College, Waltham, Massachusetts

Project Management Journal 22, no. 3 (September 1991)

WELL-DEVELOPED MANAGEMENT SKILLS are obviously vital to effective role performance of project managers, especially in today's complex, technology-oriented, highly competitive environment. Many studies have defined the type and extent of project management skills and training needed to function effectively (4) (8) (13) (15) (18). Most managers agree with the findings. Yet, their prime concern is how to develop these skills in our contemporary organizations where there is little time for "formal" training, but skills must be developed as part of an ongoing function within the organization without disrupting the current business.

In addition, funds for training and development are limited (2). Yet, another concern is for developing effective people skills and organizational skills (9) (14) (17). Traditionally, project managers were recruited and advanced primarily on the basis of the quantitative skills in such areas as planning, scheduling, cost estimating, financial controls, and critical path analysis. Equally important today, however, are the abilities to manage quality,[1] time-to-market, innovation, subcontractors, customers, and change. In addition to good technical knowledge and administrative skills, this requires leadership and people skills—that is, the ability to motivate, communicate, resolve conflict, build teams, and facilitate group decision-making. This concern is amplified in technology-oriented project environments, which involve additional risks, uncertainties, and multifunctional complexities. According to a study by the American Society for Training and Development, technical professionals are not being developed fast enough for America's needs (15). This is in spite of $125 million spent by American firms on technical/project seminars each year. Nearly half the professionals surveyed tried to improve their effectiveness in managing people. Still another concern of these managers is the selection of the "right" training method for particular skill development (4) (6) (7). While 85 percent of the managers interviewed in a field study believed that all project management skills needed for effective role performance are learnable, only 15 percent defined specific methods that they felt confident would actually develop these skills (20).

Responding to this strong interest by the project management community for assessing the effectiveness of skill development methods, several studies have investigated training techniques on a case-by-case basis (6) (17) (23). Little has been written, however, on evaluating training methods as an integrated system that employs many forms of training with various intensity over the life cycle of the career of professional managers. To close this gap, this article investigates the effectiveness of various approaches to project management training and development as perceived by managers in the field.

Objective and Method

The study is a continuation of previously published work on skill requirements for project managers (18) (19) (20), which is briefly summarized in this article. In addition, the findings from a field investigation of 220 project managers are reported. The study summarizes and evaluates the training methods used to develop the skills needed to function effectively as a project manager in today's demanding environment. Data were collected during in-house consulting assignments, based on interviews and the examination of actual training and development records. The sample includes project managers from various businesses such as computers, aerospace, tool machinery, government laboratory, and pharmaceutical. The size of the eighteen companies and business divisions in the sample varied from annual operating budgets of $2.5 million to $15 billion, averaging $375 million. These eighteen businesses run approximately 1,000 projects within one year, varying in size from a few thousand dollars to several millions.

The data evaluation and summaries rely largely on content analysis (12) of the interviews and records plus some statistical correlation analysis, using non-parametric techniques such as Kendall's Tau (16).

What Skills Do Project Managers Need?

Modern projects have become increasingly complex and multifaceted. The managers that evolve with these project organizations have to confront many challenges. They must be able to cross functional lines and deal effectively with a variety of interfaces and support personnel over whom they may have little or no formal authority. The project manager also has to cope with constant and rapid change of technology, markets, regulations, and socioeconomic factors.

What researchers find consistently and measurably (3) (8) (20) (23) (25) (26) is that project management requires skills in three primary areas—
• Leadership/interpersonal

46

- Technical, and
- Administrative—

as summarized in Table 1 and discussed below. To be effective, managers must consider all facets of the job. They must understand the people, task, tools, and organization. The days of the project manager who gets by with technical expertise alone or pure administrative skills are gone.

Interpersonal Skills and Leadership

Effective project leadership involves a whole spectrum of skills and abilities:
- Clear direction and guidance
- Ability to plan and elicit commitments
- Communication skills
- Assistance in problem solving
- Dealing effectively with managers and support personnel across functional lines, often with little or no formal authority
- Information processing skills, the ability to collect and filter relevant data valid for decision-making in a dynamic environment
- Ability to integrate individual demands, requirements, and limitations into decisions that benefit the overall project.

It further involves the project manager's ability to resolve inter-group conflicts and to build multifunctional teams.

Technical Skills

Most projects are technically complex. Project managers rarely have all the technical expertise to direct the multidisciplinary activities at hand, nor is it necessary or desirable that they do so. It is essential, however, that project managers understand the technologies and their trends, markets, and the business environment so that they can participate effectively in the search for integrated solutions and technological innovations. Without this understanding, the consequences of local decisions on the total program, the potential growth ramifications, and relationships to other business opportunities cannot be foreseen by the manager. Furthermore, technical expertise is necessary to communicate effectively with the project team and to assess risks and make tradeoffs between cost, schedule, and technical issues.

Administrative Skills

Administrative skills are essential. The project leader must be experienced in planning, staffing, budgeting, scheduling, performance evaluations, and control techniques. While it is important that managers understand the company's operating procedures and the available tools, it is often necessary for project managers to free themselves from the administrative details. Particularly for

Leadership Skill Components
Ability to manage in unstructured work environment
Clarity of management direction
Defining clear objectives
Understanding of the organization
Motivating people
Managing conflict
Understanding of professional needs
Creating personnel involvement at all levels
Communicating, written and oral
Assisting in problem solving
Aiding group decision-making
Building multidisciplinary teams
Credibility
Visibility
Gaining upper management support and commitment
Action-orientation; self-starter
Eliciting commitment
Building priority image

Technical Skill Components
Ability to manage the technology
Understanding of technology and trends
Understanding of market and product applications
Communicating with technical personnel
Fostering innovative environment
Unifying the technical team
Aiding problem solving
Facilitating tradeoffs
System perspective
Technical credibility
Integrating technical, business, and human objectives
Understanding engineering tools and support methods

Administrative Skill Components
Planning and organizing multifunctional programs
Attracting and holding quality people
Estimating and negotiating resources
Working with other organizations
Measuring work status, progress, and performance
Scheduling multidisciplinary activities
Understanding of policies and operating procedures
Delegating effectively
Communicating effectively, orally and written
Minimizing changes

Table 1. Skill Inventory of the Project Manager

larger projects, managers have to delegate considerable administrative tasks to support groups or to hire an administrator.

The project manager's effectiveness depends heavily on personal experience, credibility, and understanding of the interaction of organizational and behavioral elements. The project manager must be a social architect; that is, she must understand how the organization works and how to work with the organization. Table 1 shows a skill inventory of specific skills for each of the three primary categories. This listing was compiled from interviews with 220 project managers and is rank-ordered by the frequency at which these skills were mentioned and the perceived significance associated with effective role performance.

The significance of Table 1 is in several areas. First, it shows that the perception of skills needed by project managers in the field is very consistent with the findings of broader based research on this subject (18) (20) (21) (22). That is, today's project managers seem to be in agreement with management researchers on the skill requirements in spite of the enormous and rapid changes that the field of management is undergoing. Second, Table 1 could be used as a tool for assessing actual skill requirements and proficiencies. For example, a list could be developed, for individuals or teams, to assess for each skill component:

- Criticality of this skill to effective project performance
- Existing level of proficiency
- Potential for improvement
- Needed support systems and help
- Suggested training and development activities
- Periodic reevaluation of proficiency.

Third, Table 1 can be useful in the development of training programs, by helping focus on specific skill requirements and the development of appropriate training methods.

How Learnable Are These Skills?

Formal studies regarding the learnability of project management skills reveal some good news. On average, managers feel that 94 percent of the skills needed to perform effectively in project leadership positions are learnable.[2] As summarized in Figure 1, on-the-job experience is the largest source for developing these skills. In fact, 85 percent of all skill developments are derived from experience.[3] Three-quarters are developed strictly by experiential learning while one-quarter comes from more specific work-related methods such as observations, formal on-the-job training, upper management coaching, and job rotation. Second to experiential learning, skills can be developed by reading professional literature, such as books, magazines, journals, and research papers, as well as audio and video tapes on related subjects. A third source for project

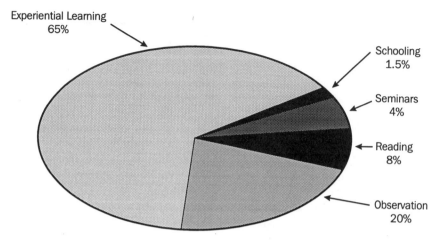

Figure 1   How Do Project Managers Develop Their Skills (Percentile indicates the perceived contribution of a method toward overall project management skills.)

management skill development exists via professional activities such as seminars, professional meetings, and special workshops. The fourth distinct category for managerial skill development consists of formal schooling. In addition, managers identify special sources, such as mentoring, job changes, and special organizational development activities for building project management skills.

The above observations are interesting and important as a basis for comparing the effectiveness of various training methods for various skills. The real significance to management is that skills can be developed. In fact, project managers point to the enormous wealth of sources available for building and developing the skills needed to perform effectively in today's demanding project environment.

How Do Organizations Train and Develop Project Managers?

Project managers are made. This is the strong conclusion reached by project managers and their superiors in our study. These managers support almost unanimously the proposition that

> project management skills don't just happen by chance but are systematically developed through formal and informal methods.

Table 2 lists the twelve most popular methods of project management skill development used by industry and government organizations. The twelve meth-

Training & Development Method		Effectiveness of			Professional Participation		
Skill Development Days	Pmgrs Days/Mgr/Yr	Leadership & People Skills	Technical Skills	Administrative Skills	%	No. of	Average
(1)		(2)			(3)	(4)	(5)
1. Experiential Learning		H	H	H	100%	64	64
2. Observing Mgmt. Practice		S	L	S	100%	10	10
3. Formal On-the-Job Training		S	H	H	8%	117	9
4. Literature Reading		L	S	L	50%	16	8
5. Coaching by Upper Mgmt.		S	L	L	15%	16	1.6
6. Seminars and Workshops		S	S	S	33%	4.6	1.5
7. Formal Courses (Degree)		S	S	S	11%	9	1
8. Consulting (Internal & External)		S	H	H	8%	12	1
9. Professional Conferences		L	S	S	27%	2.5	0.7
10. Special Work Groups		S	H	H	21%	2	0.5
11. Formal Courses (Cont. Ed.)		L	S	S	6%	5	0.3
12. Job Rotation		S	S	S	7%	?	?

Legend:

1. Training and Development Method: As defined by project managers
2. Skill Development: Primary skill areas developed as perceived by project managers
   Effectiveness Level Code:
   H—Highly effective method   **S**—Somewhat effective method   **L**—Low-effectiveness method
3. Percent participation: Percentage of project leaders participating in method (1) out of all project managers in company
4. Number of Days: The number of workdays per year spent by those project managers who participate (3) in method (1)

Table 2.   Skill Development Methods and Their Effectiveness

ods are rank-ordered by the intensity of use[4] and briefly discussed together with their effectiveness.

Experiential Learning. This is by far the most prevalent mode of skill development. All project managers seem to engage in it. On average, managers spent an equivalent of sixty-four days per year, or 25 percent of their work time, involved in on-the-job learning. It facilitates skill developments in all categories, requires little upper management supervision, and is perceived as low in cost but high in efficiency. Overall it is a very popular and effective method of project management skill development and upgrading.

Observations of Management Practice. This method has a great deal of overlap with experiential learning. However, discussions with project managers suggest a separate identity because it entails specific observations of other professionals, their actions, style, and application of management techniques.

Rather than learning from their own work experiences, managers learn from the experiences and examples set by others. This method also seems to be practiced by all project leaders. Yet, the time equivalent spent by managers observing others is only ten days per year, or 4 percent of working time. Both the cost and perceived effectiveness of this type of training is low. Further, managers point out that the effectiveness of a particular management practice is highly situational and depends on the style of the manager. What works for one manager may not produce the desired results for another. In addition, these opportunities for observing other project leaders must often be facilitated and coordinated by upper management. Yet, the benefits may be considerable. Fifty percent of the project leaders in our sample strongly believe that the observation of others is an important part of their overall managerial training and development.

Formal On-the-Job Training. This includes specific training programs, often part of a new job assignment, transfer, or new hire. The training usually consists of a combination of closely supervised work assignments, briefing sessions, and some courses, seminars, and workshops. The classroom training was estimated to be 7 percent of the total on-the-job training and is included here if it is part of a formal job training program. Only 8 percent of project management personnel are taking part in this type of training, which is costly but also highly effective, especially for those who are new to the profession.

Literature Reading. Project managers estimate that approximately 50 percent of their colleagues read professional books, journals, and reports. It is interesting to observe that all the managers interviewed stated that they would read the literature, totaling an average of sixteen working days per year (or 6.4 percent). However, for their colleagues, they estimated that only one-half would read. Both the cost and effectiveness of reading as a method for skill development are perceived low. Yet many project managers look at the literature as an important source of information and knowledge, which, through proper on-the-job application, can be transformed into skills.

Coaching by Upper Management. This seems to be a particularly effective method for skill development in the areas of team building, communications, interpersonal skills, and leadership. The relatively high cost associated with senior management involvement might limit this technique and explains its highly selective usage, an average of 1.6 days of coaching for each project manager.

Seminars and Workshops. One-third of project managers attend an average of 4.6 days of seminars per year. These could be in-plant or public offerings. At a medium cost, the overall effectiveness of these training methods is perceived at a medium level. However, in combination with experiential learning, classroom training can provide important knowledge, insight, and the foundation for accelerated skill developments, an important point that has been verified also in other studies (1).

Formal Courses (Degree Programs). Eleven percent of project managers appear to take formal courses. Although less than one-half of those who take college-level courses are actually enrolled in a degree program, managers find these courses an effective way to gain knowledge and a basis for further skill developments, especially in administration, communication, organization, planning, tracking, and measuring of project activities.

Consulting. A relatively small number of project managers (8 percent) use consulting services for skill development. Managers, who engage company internal or external experts, use their services for an average of twelve days per year. These are primarily hands-on problem solving sessions or specific assignments, such as a project start-up or recovery plan. Managers see these consulting services as effective but also costly. Those who use these services find them helpful, not only for quick problem solving but also effective for experiential learning and skill building through observation of specific techniques and practices.

Professional Conferences. Twenty-seven percent of project managers spent an average of 2.5 days each year at conferences, trade shows, and professional society meetings. These conferences are seen as vehicles for quick updates on new management concepts, techniques, support systems—such as software—and services. Equally important, project managers value the personal contacts and sharing of experiences with colleagues from other companies.

Special Work Groups. Twenty-one percent of project managers get involved in quality circles, colloquia, or other special interest work groups organized to share project management experiences and to develop the skills needed to function effectively in their organizations. Managers perceive these activities as highly effective for developing skills, especially in the more intricate areas of team building, communications, leadership, and project controls.

Formal Courses (Continuing Education). Six percent of project managers spend an average of six days each year taking formal courses. These courses are addressing the specific training needs of those enrolled; they are geared toward particular project management applications and focus on immediate applications. These courses vary in length and structure, but typically they consist of five to ten sessions at two hours each. Also included in this category are professional certification programs.

Job Rotation. Often conducted as part of formal on-the-job training, job rotation consists of a deliberate change of job category or area assignment. At a medium cost, it can be effective in developing a broad range of skills, especially those skills that require an understanding of the culture and value systems of particular organizations and job assignments.

Implications for Managers and Professional Development Specialists

Taken together, each training method has its own strengths and limitations for developing specific project management skills. However, training methods are seldom being used exclusively but rather in a combination of several methods. This can result in substantial synergism. For example, classroom training in combination with readings and on-the-job experiential learning might be an excellent way to build skill in any category and at any performance level.

The significance of our study is in three areas. First, it shows the relative effectiveness and cost of various training methods. This enables managers to fine-tune professional development programs for their people or for themselves depending on the specific job requirements. Second, it shows the relative distribution of time and effort across the various training methods that can provide some guidelines for designing professional training and development programs. Third, it stimulates thinking, regarding the type of specific training and development methods that are available.

Effective managers know the type of training and development methods available. They also seem to have a sixth sense in selecting the right combination and intensity of training that produces optimal results for the specific situation at hand. Above all, the effective manager is a social architect who understands the organization, its culture and value systems, its business environment, and technology. This is the manager who knows which type of skills is needed for successful project management and can stimulate and facilitate such professional developments and growth. An important factor in developing these needed skills is management's ability to foster a work environment conducive to their people's professional needs.

Job satisfaction and career growth are great catalysts for professional development. Managers should determine the professional ambitions of their personnel and help them attain their goals through specific work assignments, on-the-job training, and career planning and counseling and by providing development opportunities in a variety of ways. Only those people intrinsically motivated to learn and grow will truly benefit from the professional development activities available to them.

Suggestions for Developing Project Management Skills

A number of specific suggestions may be helpful in developing the skills needed for effective project management performance. Many of these suggestions are also aimed at those professionals who wish to prepare themselves for project management assignments. They are as follows:
- Observe the management practices of others.
- Develop sensitivity to what works and what does not in your own management style and environment.
- Understand available tools and techniques, especially in the administrative and technical area, via readings, courses, seminars, and workshops.
- Attend some project management-related seminars, workshops, and courses, as they provide insight into the drivers and barriers to effective management.

Such education can provide "how-to" guidelines for effective leadership, team building, communication, and conflict resolutions.

- Form a managerial interest group that meets regularly, similar to a Quality Circle, discussing specific problems and challenges, as well as techniques, to deal with them.
- Attend professional meetings, conferences, and symposia, as they can be effective forums for sharing experiences and gaining new knowledge and insight.
- Consider job rotation, either as part of a formal training program or internship, or on an ad hoc basis. It can be helpful in building and fine-tuning managerial skills.
- Solicit counseling and coaching by upper management or an outside expert.
- Perform a formal analysis of the managerial skills required in your work environment. It can provide valuable insight and suggestions for development.
- Maintain technical fitness, as it is an important prerequisite for getting the opportunity for large managerial responsibility and skill development. Therefore, staying current regarding the technologies, products, markets, and customer applications seems vital to the manager's credibility with upper management, peers, and subordinates, and ultimately for the opportunity for further career growth.
- Continue your education as a life-long learner in the job-related areas of technology, administration, and management. It is a prerequisite for managerial skill building and career development.

A Final Note

Managing projects in today's competitive environment is a highly complex, innovative, and multidisciplinary task. Project managers must have the skill to unify multifunctional teams, leading them toward integrated results. They must understand the interaction of organizational and behavioral elements in order to exert the influence required for building an environment conducive to the team's motivational needs. They must foster a climate of active participation and minimal detrimental conflict. The effective flow of communications is one of the major factors determining the quality of the organizational environment. Therefore, these managers must provide a high degree of leadership in unstructured environments.

Furthermore, the proper skills will help the project manager to develop credibility among the peer group, team members, senior management, and the customer community. Above all, these skills will help the project manager to become a social architect who understands his organization, its culture and value system, its environment, and its technology. These are the prerequisites for developing and fine-tuning the management skills needed for building a project organization toward long-range, continuous productivity improvement, and high quality standards.

Endnotes

1. In their search for ways to improve organizational effectiveness, many companies have applied total quality management concepts also to their project organizations [see references (24) (25) (26)]. Under this umbrella, continuous project management skill updating and development becomes a vital part of a company's total quality management efforts and should be integrated accordingly.

2. The manager's claim that most of these skills are learnable was verified earlier via a field study by Thamhain and Wilemon (20), which identified seven skill categories:

- Technical expertise
- Organizational skills
- Administrative skills
- Leadership
- Team building
- Interpersonal skills
- Conflict resolution skills.

On the average, 94 percent of these skills are learnable, as perceived by project managers. The learning proficiency varies depending on the particular category. For example, conflict resolution skills seem to be more difficult to learn than administrative skills. However, all categories taken together, 94 percent of project management skills seem to be learnable.

3. The percentile was determined as follows. Project leaders were asked to indicate, for each of the nine skill categories shown on the bottom of Table 2:

- What training methods helped to develop each skill
- How effective was the method
- What approximate contribution a method made to a skill development, relative to other methods employed.

A combination of questionnaires and interviews were used to collect the data, which were summarized and integrated to determine the relative contribution made by each of the five methods to leadership, technical, and administrative skill development. The distribution of sources was somewhat similar for all three skills. Figure 1 presents an aggregated view of the sources for managerial skill development.

4. Intensity is defined as the average number of days per year spent per project leader developing these skills. Managers estimate that, on the average, project leaders spend each year ninety-eight out of 250 working days developing and upgrading their skills; that amounts to 39 percent of regular working time. Equally impressive is the fact that 85 percent of the skill training and development relies on experiential methods, which include primarily on-the-job learning plus observations, formal on-the-job training, and upper management

coaching. It also includes a small amount of job rotation. The actual number of days dedicated to job rotation could not be estimated with any confidence during the field study, since the training method itself does not require any extra time but represents an ongoing work assignment in a different functional or business area. The "cost of participation" would be the transition time and effort required to change from one job assignment to another, which is clearly an area for future research. For the time being, job rotation is being treated as part of experiential learning.

References

1. Adams, John R., and Nicki S. Kirchof. 1983. A Training Technique for Developing Project Managers. *Project Management Quarterly* (March).

2. Aquilino, J.J. 1977. Multi-Skilled Work Teams: Productivity Benefits. *California Management Review* (Summer).

3. Badawy, Michael K. 1982. *Developing Managerial Skills in Engineers and Scientists.* New York: Van Nostrand Reinhold.

4. Barker, Jeffrey, Dean Tjosvold, and Robert I. Andrews. 1988. Conflict Approaches of Effective and Ineffective Project Managers: A Field Study in a Matrix Organization. *Journal of Management Studies* (UK) (March).

5. Bowenkamp, Robert D., and Brian H. Kleiner. 1987. How to Be a Successful Project Manager. *Industrial Management & Data Systems* (UK) (March/April).

6. Carter, Norman H. 1986. Career Development: A New Look. *EDP Analyser* (April).

7. ———. 1988. The Project Manager: An Emerging Professional. *Journal of Information Systems Management* (Fall).

8. Einsiedel Jr., Albert A. 1987. Profile of Effective Project Managers. *Project Management Journal* (December).

9. Gemmill, Gary R., and Hans J. Thamhain. 1973. The Effectiveness of Different Power Styles of Project Managers in Gaining Project Support. *IEEE Transactions on Engineering Management* (May).

———. 1974. The Effectiveness of Different Power Styles of Project Management in Gaining Project Support. *Project Management Quarterly* (Spring).

10. Kerzner, Harold. 1987. In Search of Excellence in Project Management. *Journal of Systems Management* (February).

11. Kezsbom, Deborah S. 1988. Leadership and Influence: The Challenge of Project Management. *AACE Transactions.*

12. Krippendorff, Klaus. 1986. *Content Analysis: An Introduction.* Sage Publications.

13. Posner, Barry Z. 1987. What It Takes to Be a Good Project Manager. *Project Management Journal* (March).

14. Rafael, Israel Dror, and Albert H. Rubenstein. 1984. Top Management Roles in R&D Projects. *R&D Management.* (UK) (January).

15. Schlick, James D. 1988. Developing Project Management Skills. *Training & Development Journal* (May).

16. Siegel, S. 1956. *Nonparametric Statistics for the Behavioral Sciences.* McGraw-Hill.

17. Syrett, Michael. 1988. New Paths for Project Management. *Director.* (UK) (January).

18. Thamhain, Hans J. 1983. Managing Engineers Effectively. *IEEE Transactions on Engineering Management* (August).

19. Thamhain, Hans J., and David L. Wilemon. 1983. Leadership Effectiveness in Project Management. In *Tutorial: Software Management*, edited by Donald J. Reifer. Los Angeles: IEEE Computer Society.

20. Thamhain, Hans J., and David L. Wileman. 1978. Skill Requirements of Engineering Program Manager. *Convention Record*, 26th Joint Engineering Management Conference (Oct.).

21. Thamhain, Hans J. 1991. Developing Engineering/Program Management Skills. Chapter in *Management of R&D and Engineering*. Wiley.

22. Thamhain, Hans J. 1990. Managing Technology: The People Factor. *Technical & Skill Training* (Aug.).

23. Thomas, Rick, and Robert Drury. 1988. Team Communication in Complex Projects. *Engineering Management International* (Netherlands) (Jan.).

24. Thornberry, Neal E. 1987. Training the Engineer as Project Manager. *Training & Development Journal* (Oct.)

25. Walsh, John J., and Jerome Kanter. 1988. Toward More Successful Project Management. *Journal of Systems Management* (Jan.).

26. Woodard, William A., and Pamela Miller. 1988. 10 Ways to Make Sure Your Projects Succeed. *Working Woman* (Dec.).

Learning to Lead, to Create Quality, to Influence Change in Projects

Lee A. Peters, Peters & Company, Zionsville, Indiana
John Homer, BMW Constructors, Indianapolis, Indiana

Project Management Journal (March 1996)

TEACHING THE CRAFT of any profession is a continuing challenge. In project management, we rely on a combination of self-discovery and apprenticeship to teach the craft of managing projects. Ultimately, a new project manager learns by observing, by being coached, and by doing.

The paradox still exits: how to produce a mission-capable project manager in a relatively short time. Project managers are anointed overnight with little attention given to prior skill development. These skills are paramount because three of five crucial developmental assignments in executive growth are projects (1).

We learned from the quality movement that a deep understanding of the processes leads to quicker learning and more consistent results—accomplishing the processes is mission capability. Project management has been aided by documentation and dissemination of successful functions but this addresses only a portion of the craft to be learned.

As with any complex craft, the selection process for the new generation of project managers is inhibited by the lack of dedicated practitioners willing or able to act as coaches and mentors, the scarcity of opportunity to personally observe poor as well as good examples of project leadership, and the time lags in projects that de-couple a clear connection between cause and effect. The result of our informal apprenticeship programs is to teach corporate culture and process better than the project craft and process.

The authors have developed a series of focused, short-interval simulations to provide multiple laboratory experiences for learning key integrated project skills. Join us on the journey to becoming a mission-capable project manager.

The Challenge

Through the design and incorporation into course materials of a series of experiential model-building simulations, we have increased the effectiveness and intensity of project management training. These simulations are cost effective for groups, use readily available technology, and automatically involve all participants in the course.

The participants experience a wide range of project processes in an environment where they directly experience the impact of team effectiveness. They can see immediate results from investment in team building and work through the consequences of their shared decisions. During the course of the simulations, various leadership and project control strategies are tested in a marketplace of ideas, and the benefits and pitfalls of alliances and of building relationships become clear.

We have used experiential simulations with contractors, project management professionals from different backgrounds, a major corporation's central engineering group, and partnering sessions with government officials and contractors.

The challenge of project management training is to accelerate learning the craft, something not normally possible on the job. The mechanics of the craft are relatively easy to learn—we sense that *scheduling* is perceived by many to be *project management*. While scheduling packages are always a hot topic at Project Management Institute meetings, the art of project management—the craft itself—is far more difficult to learn, to internalize, and then to apply.

We believe that there are three skills in that craft—that art: leadership, creating quality, and influencing change. These are tough to teach, much less learn. Like selling, schools do not teach leadership; instead they offer marketing and organizational behavior. Quality is taught statistically—quantitatively but not qualitatively, other than in outside courses such as analytical chemistry. Change control is preached, but only the books on crisis management approach any aspect of influencing change (2). Change happens with or without control. We can influence but never actually control change, not unlike the way California controls earthquakes. The effect, not the affect, is mitigated.

Learn to Do Without

There is, however, a profession that addresses all three: the military, "the profession of arms." The military, more so than any other organization, practices or rehearses its craft (3). People are forever training to accomplish hypothetical missions. Real experience (making mistakes) is obtained in a thousand ways without actual combat experience. Command post exercises, field maneuvers, battle drills, live fire, logistical exercises, training exercises without troops, terrain walks, staff rides, sand tables, map exercises, and war gaming are but a few of the ways experience is obtained. What do we in project management do that is comparable?

How are change, quality, and leadership integrated and internalized? How will we intuitively respond to the "fog" of battle during the project?

In human endeavor, project management and war have much in common: moving resources to achieve a business objective is nearly identical to moving units to attain a military objective. Like war, the project environment is a harsh world—mistakes are rapidly punished, messengers are shot, and blame is placed everywhere else. And there may be casualties, because the fallout from a mismanaged project can be as traumatic—or fatal—as a battlefield wound.

So, how do you accelerate the learning curve and make the learning less risky? More importantly, how can we change values and behaviors so that the project terrain is less dangerous and more nurturing? How do you teach different or new concepts such as total quality management?

The answer is in *simulations*—war games. Chess is a war game that has become a part of the human psyche (4). War gaming kept several German generals out of the Normandy Invasion (5). An early commercial war game issued during Desert Shield proved that Desert Storm would only take four days (6).

Project managers use simulations already. The ever-present critical path technique (CPM) is a simulation (7). Using this static technique to simulate the dynamic project, project managers build the project on paper before it is built on the ground. The process of doing in private before doing in public helps the team learn the project, issues, goals, and relationships before ever beginning the project. The CPM then becomes a control tool—actually a re-simulation device where the logic, the reality, the progress, can all be revisited and reworked—before it happens in real time.

What benefit do simulations have over other forms of training? Project management courses can be dry, lecture-intensive learning environments. The best environment is to learn while "under fire." People learn project management skills on the job—by doing, by struggle, and by evaluating good and bad actions.

Simulations do accelerate learning—consider the Apollo Project without the thousands of simulated practices. Project cycle times can be reduced and, by experiencing many cycles of learning, people can more quickly become excellent managers. We believe that simulation—a make-believe reality—is the tool to increase the efficiency of the learning environment.

Simulation Creation

Our original model-building application evolved as an approach to teach the total quality management concepts of process improvement to construction people. We developed the idea from an experience twenty years earlier with a simulation, *Lego®MAN:* a single-purpose simulation that taught the value of investing in teams and a mission versus investing in a person with a job function (8). We continued to explore and to develop simulations that greatly enhanced learning, leadership, quality, and change (see side bar, "Project Quality Improvement").

Project Quality Improvement

In the first application of this technology, a series of simulations was employed to provide experience in the total quality management concepts of continuous improvement as applied to project management. The exercises were performed within a construction company by teams of employees from throughout the organization.

In this set of exercises, eight teams competitively built three successive models over a period of weeks. Scoring was published as each round was completed. Scoring was cost-based with costs incurred on materials, planning time, construction time (at a different rate), and the cost of optional services obtained from the facilitator. The exercises shared technology and ground rules but were distinct exercises.

In common with construction processes generally, the key to success was in recognizing and improving the core processes common to the projects. No one project allowed for a sufficiently detailed plan to optimize fully for those aspects unique to the specific project. Team effectiveness grew markedly across the course of the three exercises.

In the scoring of this set of exercises each team improved on each repetition from their previous performance. This improvement culminated in the best team performance requiring approximately one-tenth of the time required for that team's original performance. The winning team split a prize of $100.

Of interest to report was the result of using a modified simulation in a superintendents' meeting. In this use, four performing teams were each seeded with one person, in each case a young engineer, who had participated in the previous contest. Every team ceded leadership to this experienced person. The "experienced" leader then helped his team produce a very poor estimate of their cost of performance, resulting in an unprofitable contract. Seemingly, these young, strongly task-oriented engineers remembered their previous simulation experience more clearly in terms of the final score. Forgotten were the lessons of effective planning and team building by which they earned that score.

From these experiences we developed an ice-breaking simulation that has been used many times. Invariably this exercise results in opportunities to observe good and bad team interactions. We observe planning efforts to receive lip service but no effective effort. The teams usually are inefficient in the employment of resources, waste considerable time, and suffer the impact of haste or of selected strategies that prove ineffective.

Almost without exception the team will take much longer to construct the model than would be expected of a single individual. Usually they will suffer quality problems in their first attempt to gain acceptance of their submission. Rarely has a team been able to perform within the offered contract price.

We searched for supplementary means of modeling project team interactions that would build on shared experience and use experiential learning for project managers. We experimented with model-building processes as models of project interactions. The technology as developed proved successful in providing learning situations where participants can view project processes in an understandable context.

Teams are formed and given problems to solve. The problem is constrained by a time frame and, as appropriate, by a cost structure. Depending on the objectives set, focus can be developed on *intra-team cooperation, inter-team cooperation, inter-team competition, team building, decision processes*, recognizing the reality of or maximizing the effectiveness of *project overhead, project control systems, project process improvement, effective delegation*, or the *interface of teams* simultaneously working on separate aspects of the complete problem.

On Learning

Our commitment to simulations comes from the study of teaching. We discovered Malcolm Knowles, who founded the concepts of how adults learn and an adult learning process (9). The adult, and even a child in many situations, learns best by doing—by struggling. The adult learns best from peers rather than instructors. An adult—unlike children—will only learn when there is an immediate need—"just-in-time learning." Adults have a strong need to apply what they learn immediately. They are not patient enough to learn things for which they do not perceive an application. The teacher becomes a facilitator; the student is responsible for learning.

In additional leadership studies, we learned that the mind cannot differentiate between reality and fantasy (10). Psychotherapy has techniques to "change history," to relieve issues with a past cause. People can learn important lessons in an analogous environment—a metaphor.

We used a successful metaphorical learning methodology to accelerate strategic planning by taking an imaginary fishing trip or golfing vacation and relating the planning and execution of that trip to the business issues at hand (11). The metaphor released creative forces that rapidly identified and addressed business issues consistently and with clarity. The sixth-sense construct unleashed tremendous creativity, high-quality results, and long retention of the experience.

People do not have to be in the same environment to learn valuable lessons that can be applied in other settings. Nor do they have to address the same technical projects to learn project management skills. Later we learned that Edward de Bono used metaphors in his creative work—fantasy that can be stepped into and lived—like the "holodeck" on *Star Trek* (see side bar, "Learning Criteria") (12).

Growing Project Managers

The age-old question of whether a skill is inherent or acquired is still encountered concerning the skill sets of project managers. Sponsors now recognize that project managers are grown, not born. This has increased the effort directed at

Learning Criteria

We believe that the mind cannot differentiate learning in a metaphor from learning in a "real" environment. Simulations accelerate learning from experience by providing access to repeated cycles of learning.

Learning must be applied to be adopted. A learning environment that encourages experimentation and provides immediate response leads to more effective application of lessons in "real" situations. The simulations provide this fail-safe environment and build confidence for application of tools mastered.

Simulations have been structured to meet criteria we believe accelerate learning:

- Adults learn by doing. Each simulation is a team-focused activity.
- Adults learn when fully engaged. Simulations employ all senses in what universally becomes a very intense experience.
- Adults learn by struggle. Each simulation incorporates trial and error.
- Adults learn from each other. The simulations maximize individual learning through shared experience.

finding economical and effective training methods as a means of transferring knowledge and developing skills.

The diversity, scope, and complexity of the real-life situations with which they are expected to cope complicate training of project managers. This brings imposing difficulty to the issue of building effective training models within the scope and complexity limited by practicality (see side bar, "Project Teaching Mechanisms").

Experiential model-building simulations provide immediate reactions and the opportunity for multiple cycles of learning in a short time. By providing a shared experience base for all participants, identification of the application of concepts developed to real projects is often instantaneous (see side bar, "Project Management Realities and Simulations").

Our Learning

What have we learned by using experiential model-building simulations?

- Behaviors mirror project management styles; people behave in the simulation as they do in real life. Behaviors are replicated inside the simulations that were learned outside. Managers use the behaviors they believe led to prior successes. Since project management types tend to be hardworking, detail-driven, task-oriented people, we see these behaviors in the simulations where other behaviors are more appropriate.

Project Teaching Mechanisms

The first attempts at using these simulations followed the recognition that all means of training in specific aspects of project management have their place and limitations.

Lecturing can be excused as a cost-effective way to convey standardized information to an audience. In practice it works better as evidence of having given the instruction than as a means of affecting behavior.

Computer simulations make great scorekeepers, quickly projecting the impact of specific decisions and allowing exploration of alternate strategies. Reportedly an oil company was so impressed by the training opportunities they observed in SimCity®, a computer game, that they commissioned the designers to build a computer model of refinery operations as a training tool.

Computer models poorly model the team process involved in reaching decisions. These models often place an understanding of the technology (of computers) ahead of learning the lessons sought.

Case studies can provide a means for sharing experience in reaching decisions but do a poor job of modeling the impact of decisions. They lead to decision review in a very detached, academic manner, again failing to model the processes of team decision-making.

Business Week reported using *Legos®* to train teams in production changes in a GM European plant (13).

War games are gaining business interest as are other metaphorical learning experiences (14).

- Participants have to be reinforced, reminded, and encouraged to try new ways, to employ recently learned concepts. People will try on new behaviors if the environment encourages and protects the testing.
- Generally people in projects and simulations want to complete the problem and not look at underlying theory nor evaluate the experience to explore what they might have learned. They just want to get done.
- The metaphorical aspect appears to show that the creative types learn faster; the practical types have varying levels of difficulty getting inside the simulation. The "right brainers" have more degrees of freedom in being able to live differently.
- Teams do not just happen—throwing folks together does not make them a team. Teams must be built. Projects simulations can help build teams.
- Teams form strong bonds and resist being broken up; they want to perform well together. They would rather stay together than adjust to new people. The reality in the known is safer than the unknown.
- The creative juices begin to flow; the brain is freed up; the power of fantasy is valued. Learning is actually fun—the lessons embed in the subconscious because the conscious is enjoying itself.

Project Management Realities and Simulations

The experiential model-building simulations are well adapted to project realities. Through the exercises, the following realities are reinforced and internalized:

Projects are a people business. Behavior in simulations mirrors real-world behavior of participants. Changed behavior within a simulation will bring changed real-world behavior.

Relationships are the key to success in projects. The use of simulations emphasizes team building, cooperation, collaboration, and listening—particularly to the users, sponsors, and champions.

Projects run by communication. Simulations focus on requirements for clear communication (written and verbal) in understanding expectations, processes, goals, objectives, designs, and success criteria.

Effective planning pays. Emphasis on planning helps to realize the tenfold payoff in project management for effective planning. The dimensions of strategic, tactical, and operational planning are better understood after working with the concepts. Successive simulations develop complex planning skills.

Time is a perishable resource. Emphasis on time limits in simulations develops understanding of using time effectively.

Projects are won by processes. Many processes contribute to project success. Logistics, procurement, risk management, performance contract, time organization, cost accounting, knowing, seeing the process, measuring results, challenging the system, and using the process create project success.

Leadership embraces the project. Every word, every day influences the people of the project. What needs to be modeled, what empowers, what keeps people caring? Use the key skills of a project leader to develop teams, nurture people, and grow customer satisfaction. Simulations allow newly acquired leadership skills to be practiced in a fail-safe environment.

Learning and improvement must be perpetual, both within and between projects. Debriefs, planning, tool deployment, and skill building all stress continuous learning. Learning is accomplished by individuals and teams. Organizations advance through the collective learning of individuals and teams. Simulations require practice and model continuous feedback and learning. Teams learn to improve quality continuously.

- There are at least four or five kinds of project environments; projects are not all the same even within an industry. The industry-specific groups typify this. Metaphorical simulations allow people from different backgrounds to learn together.
- Complex processes and interactions, such as in a microeconomy, can be effectively modeled in a short time. These simulations bring real-world issues

into the learning situation. Participants confront competing agendas and must satisfy others to successfully complete projects—in a few hours.

- People remember the simulations and the underlying messages. Weeks later they speak of the experience and its lessons.

We learned that one simulation cannot be all encompassing. Skills can be taught and reinforced by short, quick, turnaround exercises. A single simulation can teach three or four skills. Even though the actual exercise may require ten or twelve skills, only a small set should be emphasized. We have, however, pondered about running the same simulation a second or third time to teach additional skills; that is because people are such amazingly quick learners. They are able to be successful, and they learn the rules of the game. We prefer to move people to more complex simulations comparable to real-life experience, where they have to figure out what they learned, what is pertinent to this challenge, and how to apply that learning.

The most effective teaching occurs when each exercise results in an after-action review of the exercise, tailored to specific course goals. The feedback on the skills is typically used as an introduction to specific project processes. For example, the planning failures of a first exercise can lead directly to instruction of effective planning methods.

An after-action review is a powerful means of learning from doing. We learned that we could change the focus of the simulation by what questions we asked in the debrief or by changing the preceding lessons. The objectives of the learning need to be defined and the debrief constructed to follow those objectives. It is essential that the lesson and the debrief be aligned.

A further adaptation of the technology is currently in use on a divisionwide basis in the engineering department of a major manufacturer. (See *PM Network*, September 1994.) Here it is being used to help in the training of upgraded project skills for project management and engineering personnel. In this organization, four simulations are used in a weeklong course culminating in a four-hour simulation of a microeconomy, involving team roles as owners, suppliers, engineers, and contractors.

A common theme for all the simulations is the use of a team approach to build organizational effectiveness while efficiently accomplishing the goals of the project. The simulations have proven very effective to point out the faults of project managers who too often attempt to excuse inefficiency and ineffective team action. The universal attempt to excuse such behaviors in the name of deadlines and budget constraints is demonstrated as futile. Experience with the simulations has shown that, just as in real projects, effective approaches to organizational process management yield the best long-term project results. This conclusion is not self-evident to project participants, but through the effective use of targeted simulations the lesson is absorbed.

Another consistently observed phenomenon is the disproportionate impact on project process of minor changes. Participants must learn quickly to adapt to change or else get eaten alive. One experience had an engineer dominate the simulations with negotiations for payment for minor change. When that change was granted, the group lost all creativity because of the increased time pressure—it disintegrated. In general, the impact of minor change is devastating to inexperienced teams.

Simulation methodology can be readily adapted to obtain effectiveness in teaching many project management processes. Direct examples can be drawn to help in teaching many processes: team formation, team building, effective planning, work breakdown structure, scheduling, estimating, scope definition, and incorporating project controls systems. Experience has shown this effectiveness in many environments. The simulations used to date are sufficiently generic to have found general applicability, with adaption, to many project management environments. The models have been adjusted to the needs of a variety of specific projects or performing organizations.

Summary

Simulations have been used for many years to enhance professional crafts. Aircraft simulations have a long tradition, now enhanced by computer-aided simulations, aimed at teaching skills as varied as truck driving, extra-vehicular space walking, and stomach surgery.

The craft of project management can be learned. The authors' experiences show that well-designed, small-scale project simulations can focus teams and individuals on learning critical project skills within days.

References/Endnotes

1. Lindsey, Esther H., Virginia Homes, and Morgan W. McCall Jr. 1987. *Key Events in Executives' Lives.* Technical Report Number 31 (October). Greensboro, N.C.: Center for Creative Leadership.

2. Beckhard, Richard, and Reuben T. Harris. 1987. *Organizational Transitions—Managing Complex Change.* Addison-Wesley Publishing Co.

Fink, Steven. 1987. *Crisis Management—Planning for the Inevitable.* New York: American Management Association.

Martel, Leon. 1986. *Mastering Change.* New York: New American Library.

3. Army Orders Truck Driving Simulators. 1992. *Journal of Commerce and Commercial* 394, no. 27855 (November 16): 3B.

Hamilton, Dane. 1992. Training on Truck Simulator Helps Combat Driver Shortage. *Journal of Commerce and Commercial* 393, no. 27812 (September 14): 3B.

Kolcum, Edward H. 1991. Desert Storm Highlights Need for New Training System Concepts. *Aviation Week & Space Technology* 135, no. 21 (November 25): 102.

Lesser, Roger. 1994. Military Training Systems Keying on State-of-the-Art Technology. *Defense Electronics* 26, no. 11 (November): 2A.

4. Perla, Peter P. 1990. *The Art of Wargaming: A Guide for Professionals and Hobbyist.* Annapolis, Md.: Naval Institute Press.

5. Keagen, John. 1983. *Six Armies in Normandy*. (June) New York: Penguin Books.

6. A war gaming colleague's experience with a commercial game before the ground phase began.

7. To build a CPM, one must build the project on paper. A doing without before doing with—a simulation.

8. Reddy, W. Brendon, and Otto Kroeger. 1972. Intergroup Model-Building: The Lego®Man. *The 1972 Annual Handbook for Group Facilitators*. University Associates.

9. Knowles, Malcolm S., and Associates. 1984. *Andragogy in Action—Applying Modern Principles of Adult Learning*. San Francisco: Jossey-Bass, Inc.

10. Thirty books on neurolinguistic programming (NLP) and psychotherapy.

11. Personal experience at two conferences and with Chamber of Commerce training.

12. DeBono, Edward. 1970. *Lateral Thinking: Creativity Step by Step*. New York: Harper & Row.

13. Ingrassia, Paul, and Joseph B. White. 1994. *Comeback: The Fall and Rise of the American Automobile Industry*. New York: Simon & Schuster.

Miller, Karen Lowry. 1993. GM's German Lessons. *Business Week*, no. 3351 (December): 67.

14. Johnstone, Bob. 1991. Modeling the Future. *Far Eastern Economic Review* 153, no. 32 (August 8): 70.

Szwergold, Jack. 1994. When Work Has You Climbing Trees. *Management Review* 82, no. 9 (December 12): 6.

Bulkeley, William M. 1994. Business War Games Attract Big Warriors. *Wall Street Journal* (December 12).

Situational Leadership in a Project/Matrix Environment

Nicholas DiMarco, Senior Consultant and Director of Program Development,
Human Resource Management Corporation
Jane R. Goodson, Department of Management, Auburn University at Montgomery
Henry F. Houser, Department of Management, Auburn University at Montgomery

Project Management Journal 20, no. 1 (March 1989)

THE SET OF complex circumstances facing project managers creates a unique managerial role. Even under the simplest of organizational structures, the project manager must possess skills in communication, integration, negotiation, and team-building (2) (7). These skills are essential for successful project management, despite the fact that most project managers have advanced from the technical ranks and, as a result, have received little management training (5). Under the more complex structure in which project managers typically operate—the matrix organization—an even wider range of leadership skills is needed to bring about project success. This paper provides an approach for identifying leader behaviors and skills that are important to effectiveness in a matrix/project environment.

The matrix structure is a mechanism by which to maximize the benefits of the functional and project forms of organization, while minimizing their disadvantages (4). The ability to choose the disciplinary "mix" of skills needed for a particular project allows for maximum flexibility and effectiveness. However, the dual lines of supervision created by such a structure also translate into a complex managerial situation.

A major issue arising out of the dual supervision of matrix structures is whether or not the project manager will have the influence necessary to bring about the successful completion of the project. According to Katz and Allen (4), individuals in a project team will respond to the manager (project or functional) whom they perceive to have the greatest control over technical decisions, salary and promotion decisions, and/or staffing assignments. As a result, skills in procuring valued resources for individual team members would become crucial to effective project leadership. This would not only require that project managers be aware of their own team members' needs and expectations but also skillful in building influence networks outside the project team.

The dual lines of responsibility arising from matrix structures also may create uncertainty or ambiguity regarding the roles of project managers (3). This, in combination with joint decision-making, competition for scarce resources, and different values and objectives that characterize the matrix organization makes skills in conflict management essential for the project leader. Project managers, however, may not understand the risks and consequences of conflict or how to deal with it (6). More participative modes of conflict resolution, such as confrontation and problem solving, may be needed to encourage individuals to work together for project success (3).

It is clear that the leadership skills required of project managers are diverse. However, there is less understanding of the specific kinds of leadership roles that both project and functional managers should assume in order to most effectively support matrix relationships. Dilworth et al. (1) suggested that the roles of project and functional managers should vary according to the particular project and/or environmental situation. This situational approach is consistent with the current thinking in the area of leadership/management development. Specifically, the situational approach to leadership/management asserts that the best way to manage or supervise depends on the environment in which a manager functions.

Thus, an assessment of the management situation is first undertaken, and, in response, various managerial behaviors are prescribed.

Purpose

This paper describes the application of a situational management training program for project managers and functional managers of a large project-oriented engineering department of a national production company. The engineering department oversees the design and construction of large capital products for the company. The steps included a situational assessment of management needs from the perspectives of project managers, project team members, functional managers, and functional staff members; an assessment of the present skill levels of project and functional managers from the perspectives of all four groups; and an identification of the areas to be targeted for management development.

Method

Situational Assessment

A model developed by Yukl (8) provided the framework by which to determine the management needs of the project managers and functional managers. This

1. **Performance Emphasis**: the need to emphasize the importance of subordinate performance, improve productivity and efficiency, keep subordinates working up to their capacities, and check on performance.

2. **Consideration**: the need to be friendly, supportive, and considerate in behavior toward subordinates and to be fair and objective.

3. **Inspiration**: the need to stimulate enthusiasm among subordinates for the work of the group and to say things that build confidence in subordinates' abilities to perform assignments successfully.

4. **Praise-Recognition**: the need to provide praise and recognition to subordinates who perform effectively, to show appreciation for their special efforts and contributions, and to make sure they get credit for their helpful ideas and suggestions.

5. **Structuring Reward Contingencies**: the need to reward effective subordinate performance with tangible benefits, such as pay increases, promotions, more desirable assignments, better work schedules, more time off, and so on.

6. **Decision Participation**: the need to consult with subordinates and to otherwise allow them to influence managerial decisions.

7. **Autonomy-Delegation**: the need to delegate authority and responsibility to subordinates and allow them to determine how to do their work.

8. **Role Clarification**: the need to inform subordinates about their duties and responsibilities, specify the rules and policies that must be observed, and let subordinates know what is expected of them.

9. **Goal Setting:** the need to emphasize the importance of setting specific performance goals for each important aspect of a subordinate's job, measure progress toward the goals, and provide concrete feedback.

10. **Training-Coaching**: the need to determine training needs for subordinates, and to provide any necessary training and coaching.

11. **Information Dissemination**: the need to keep subordinates informed about developments that affect their work, including events in other work units or outside the organization, decisions made by higher management, and progress in meetings with superiors or outsiders.

12. **Problem Solving**: the need to take the initiative in proposing solutions to serious work-related problems and act decisively to deal with such problems when a prompt solution is needed.

13. **Planning**: the need to organize efficiently and schedule the work in advance, plan how to attain work unit objectives, and make contingency plans for potential problems.

14. **Coordination**: the need to coordinate the work of subordinates, emphasize the importance of coordination, and encourage subordinates to coordinate their activities.

15. **Work Facilitation**: the need to obtain for subordinates any of the necessary supplies, equipment, support service, or other resources; eliminate problems in the work environment; and remove other obstacles that interfere with the work.

16. **Representation**: the need to establish contacts with other groups and important people in the organization, persuade them to appreciate and support the supervisor's work unit, and to use influence with superiors and outsiders to promote and defend the interests of the work unit.

17. **Interaction Facilitation**: the need to try to get subordinates to be friendly with each other, cooperate, share information and ideas, and help one another.

18. **Conflict Management**: the need to restrain subordinates from fighting and arguing, encourage them to resolve conflicts in a constructive manner, and help to settle conflicts and disagreements between subordinates.

19. **Criticism-Discipline**: the need to constructively criticize or discipline a subordinate who shows consistently poor performance, violates a rule, or disobeys an order; disciplinary actions include an official warning, reprimand, suspension, or dismissal.

Figure 1 Situational Needs Dimensions

Instructions: To what extent do the following conditions apply or occur in the area/department/project team you manage or are a member of?

1. *Never (not at all)*
2. *Seldom (to a limited extent)*
3. *Sometimes (to a moderate extent)*
4. *Usually (to a considerable extent)*
5. *Always (to a very great extent)*

1. Team member errors and quality deficiencies would endanger the health and lives of people or be costly and difficult to correct.
2. The manager's unit is in direct competition with other units or organizations, and it can survive and prosper only by being more efficient and productive than competitors.
3. The manager's unit is highly interdependent with other units in the organization. Failure to meet deadlines or achieve planned levels of output or services would seriously disrupt other units' activities.
4. The manager is under extreme pressure from higher management, directors, or owners to increase profits, improve productivity, reduce costs, or otherwise improve the unit's performance.
5. Team members are not highly motivated to do the work and are likely to "slack off" if not prodded and encouraged.

Figure 2   Items Used to Assess the Performance Emphasis Need

model builds on and takes into account the shortcomings of earlier leadership models and provides a more comprehensive approach to situational management development. Specifically, the model identifies a variety of leader behaviors and specifies conditions under which the use of each of these behaviors would maximize leader effectiveness. In this model, factors such as the following are important in determining the needs of a particular situation: the nature of the people managed (e.g., project members' understanding of job duties and responsibilities); the nature of projects performed (e.g., variety in projects); the nature of the influence structure (e.g., authority and discretion of the individual project and functional managers); and the nature of the organizational climate (e.g., project manager-project member relations, functional manager-project member relations, intra- and inter-staff relations). A detailed analysis of these factors resulted in the identification of nineteen "needs" that the project manager and/or functional manager may be required to manage. These needs are described in Figure 1.

The Situational Assessment Questionnaire (SAQ) was used to determine the magnitude of each need. The SAQ was administered to both project managers and their subordinate team members and functional managers and their subordinates. Each manager-subordinate team was coded. The average for all the staff members reporting to a given manager was used in the analysis. The items

MANAGERIAL FORM—COMPLETED BY MANAGER

Instructions: For each item, please select the answer that best describes your managerial behavior. Please put the number of that answer on the line in front of the item. The answer choices are as follows:

1. Never (not at all)
2. Seldom (to a limited extent)
3. Sometimes (to a moderate extent)
4. Usually (to a considerable extent)
5. Always (to a very great extent)

Performance Emphasis

1. I emphasize the importance of achieving a high level of performance.
2. I try to keep team members working at their maximum level of performance.
3. I push for increased effectiveness and efficiency.
4. I encourage team members to do high quality work.

TEAM MEMBER FORM—COMPLETED BY A SAMPLE OF 3–5 TEAM MEMBERS

1. My manager emphasizes the importance of achieving a high level of performance.
2. My manager tries to keep team members working at their maximum levels of performance.
3. My manager pushes for increased effectiveness and efficiency.
4. My manager encourages team members to do high quality work.

Figure 3   Manager Behavior Description Questionnaire Items Assessing
Performance Emphasis

that comprised one need dimension, the Performance Emphasis Need dimension, are presented in Figure 2. The more the conditions described in Figure 2 were present in the environment in which managers and subordinates operated (the higher the scores), the stronger the need for performance emphasis. The remaining eighteen need dimensions were similarly assessed.

Assessment of Present Skill Level

The second step in the situational management development model was to evaluate how well the project and functional managers were presently performing on the nineteen dimensions identified in the SAQ. This was determined by having the project managers and their team members, and the functional managers and their subordinates, complete the Manager/Supervisor Behavioral Description Questionnaire (BDQ). There are two forms for the BDQ—one completed by the project and functional managers and one by their respective subordinates. There is a third form that can be completed by the superiors of the project and functional managers; however, it was not used in this study.

DIMENSIONS	FUNCTIONAL MANAGER MEAN	SD	SUB. MEAN	SD	PROJECT MANAGER MEAN	SD	SUB. MEAN	SD	DIFFERENCES F-VALUE	BETWEEN GROUPS+
1. Performance Emphasis	3.4	.8	3.3	.7	3.8	.5	3.5	.9	2.8*	2-3
2. Consideration	2.2	.6	2.8	.6	2.6	.4	2.8	.8	5.4***	1-2, 3, 4
3. Inspiration	2.9	.7	2.7	.8	2.6	.5	2.9	.7	1.9	
4. Praise-Recognition	2.8	.6	3.0	.7	3.0	.7	3.2	.7	2.6*	1-4
5. Structuring Reward Contingencies	2.6	.7	2.8	.6	3.0	.5	3.1	.6	6.3***	1-3, 4 2-4
6. Decision Participation	4.0	.6	4.2	.7	3.8	.6	4.2	.7	2.7*	2-3, 3-4
7. Autonomy-Delegation	3.6	.7	3.9	.6	3.7	.6	4.0	.6	3.4*	1-4, 3-4
8. Role Clarification	2.6	.6	2.5	.6	2.4	.6	2.5	.7	.4	
9. Goal Setting	3.9	.6	3.7	.8	3.7	.7	3.5	.8	2.1	1-4
10. Training-Coaching	3.1	.7	2.9	.6	2.8	.6	2.6	.7	5.2**	1-4, 2-4
11. Information Dissemination	3.2	.8	3.5	.7	3.8	.7	3.9	.7	8.6***	1-3, 4 2-4
12. Problem Solving	3.0	.7	2.8	.6	2.7	.7	2.9	.8	1.0	
13. Planning	3.4	.6	3.4	.7	3.8	.7	3.5	.7	2.2	2-3
14. Coordination	3.4	.6	3.7	.6	3.8	.6	3.9	.8	3.6**	1-4
15. Work Facilitation	3.2	.8	3.4	.7	3.0	.7	2.9	.7	8.1***	2-3, 4
16. Representation	3.4	.6	3.8	.5	3.9	.6	4.2	.7	13.2***	1-2, 3, 4 2-4, 3-4
17. Interaction Facilitation	3.4	.6	3.5	.6	3.7	.7	3.8	.8	3.8**	1-4, 2-4
18. Conflict Management	2.4	.7	2.3	.5	2.6	.5	2.4	.6	1.8	2-3
19. Criticism-Discipline	2.6	.7	2.5	.6	2.8	.5	2.6	.6	1.6	

+ Differences Between the Means for the Groups are Significantly Different Beyond the .05 Level (Duncan's New Multiple Range Test)

*P.<<05 **P<<.01 ***P<<.001

Table 1. Means and Standard Deviations for Situational Need Dimension Scores for Functional and Project Managers and Their Subordinates and F-Values for the Comparisons between Groups

Figure 3 presents the items comprising the Performance Emphasis dimension. The performance emphasis scale represents those management behaviors necessary to ensure the high productivity, efficiency, and quality required by the situation. The remaining eighteen dimensions were similarly assessed.

Areas Targeted for Management Development

Areas in greatest need of change and/or development were identified by combining the results of the situational needs and managerial behavior/skill level assessments. The matching of needs and behaviors resulted in three outcomes for each dimension:

1. Behavior/skill level needed to be increased because it was lower than the need level.

2. Behavior/skill level needed to be decreased because it was higher than the need level.

3. Behavior/skill level should remain the same because it matched the need level.

Results

As part of the training effort, both project and functional managers were encouraged to provide feedback to their subordinates on the results of the study. Each manager presented the results to his own employees.

Table 1 presents the means and standard deviations of the need scores from the perspectives of functional managers (n = 34), subordinates of functional managers (n = 122), project managers (n = 22), and subordinates of project managers (n = 88). The overall F-value provided in Table 1 indicated whether or not statistically significant differences between the means of two or more of the four groups existed. However, this test cannot identify which groups have significantly different mean values. Duncan's Multiple Range test compared all possible pairs of the means of the four groups to identify the specific groups that had significantly different mean values.

Table 1 indicates that there were twelve need dimensions with significant F-values. The Duncan Multiple Range Test compared all the mean scores for all four groups. For the purpose of this study, significant differences between functional managers and their staff members (groups 1 and 2), project managers and their team members (groups 3 and 4), functional managers and project managers (groups 1 and 3), and functional staff members and project team members (groups 2 and 4) were examined.

A comparison of functional managers and their staff members (groups 1 and 2) showed that staff members' scores were significantly higher on the consideration and representation dimensions. Project team members had significantly higher scores than project managers on the Decision-Participation, Autonomy-Delegation, and Representation dimensions.

A comparison of functional and project managers (groups 1 and 3, respectively) indicated that project managers' scores were significantly higher on the Consideration, Structuring Reward Contingencies, Information Dissemination, and Representation dimensions.

Lastly, a comparison of functional staff members and project team members (groups 2 and 4, respectively) showed that functional staff members had significantly higher scores on the Training-Coaching and Work Facilitation dimensions, while project team members had significantly higher scores on the Structuring Reward Contingencies, Information Dissemination, Representation, and Interaction Facilitation dimensions.

	FUNCTIONAL				PROJECT				
	MANAGER		SUB.		MANAGER		SUB. DIFFERENCES		
DIMENSIONS	MEAN	SD	MEAN	SD	MEAN	SD	MEAN	SD	F-VALUE BETWEEN GROUPS+
1. Performance Emphasis	4.5	.4	4.4	.5	3.9	.7	4.1	.6	2.1	
2. Consideration	4.1	.8	3.2	.7	4.0	.8	3.3	.7	4.6**	1-2, 3-4
3. Inspiration	4.9	.7	3.0	.7	3.7	.7	3.1	.8	4.7**	1-2
4. Praise-Recognition	4.2	.6	3.3	.6	4.0	.6	3.1	.9	7.1***	1-2, 3-4
5. Structuring Reward Contingencies	3.8	.5	3.2	.7	3.9	.7	3.2	.7	4.2**	3-4
6. Decision Participation	4.4	.5	3.6	.6	4.2	.7	3.1	.8	10.9***	1-2, 2-4, 3-4
7. Autonomy-Delegation	4.5	.4	3.9	.7	4.2	.7	3.6	.7	8.8***	1-2, 2-4, 3-4
8. Role Clarification	4.2	.7	4.0	.7	4.0	.7	3.7	.8	3.1*	2-4
9. Goal Setting	4.3	.6	3.9	.6	4.1	.8	3.8	.8	2.5*	1-2
10. Training-Coaching	3.7	.7	3.1	.5	3.8	.7	3.5	.7	4.2**	1-2, 2-4
11. Information Dissemination	4.3	.6	3.2	.7	4.2	.7	3.3	.6	9.8***	1-2, 3-4
12. Problem Solving	4.4	.4	3.7	.6	4.0	.8	3.6	.7	4.8**	1-2
13. Planning	1.3	.6	3.6	.5	3.9	.7	3.5	.8	4.9**	1-2
14. Coordination	4.6	.3	4.0	.7	3.8	.6	3.2	.7	7.7***	1-2, 1-3, 2-4, 3-4
15. Work Facilitation	4.0	.6	3.7	.8	4.1	.5	3.8	.6	2.6*	3-4
16. Representation	4.3	.5	3.2	.7	4.2	.6	3.1	.7	9.2***	1-2, 3-4
17. Interaction Facilitation	4.5	.4	3.3	.6	4.0	.5	3.2	.6	8.7***	1-2, 3-4
18. Conflict Management	4.0	.5	3.1	.7	3.8	.6	3.2	.7	4.0**	1-2
19. Criticism-Discipline	3.2	.6	3.0	.6	3.4	.7	3.1	.6	.6	

+ Differences Between the Means for the Groups are Significantly Different Beyond the .05 Level (Duncan's New Multiple Range Test)

*P<<.05 **P<<.01 ***P<<.001

Table 2. Means and Standard Deviations for Behavioral Dimension Scores for Functional and Project Managers and Their Subordinates and F-Values for the Comparisons between Groups

Table 2 presents the means, standard deviations, and F-values of the managerial behavior scores for all four groups. The table indicates that on seventeen of the nineteen dimensions there were significant differences between the various groups. An examination of the results in Table 2 will show that they parallel the presentation for Table 1.

A comparison of functional managers and their staff members (groups 1 and 2) and project managers and their team members (groups 3 and 4) indicated that both groups of managers had significantly higher scores than their respective staff members on the Consideration, Praise-Recognition, Decision Participation, Autonomy-Delegation, and Information Dissemination, Coordination, Representation, and Interaction Facilitation dimensions. In addition, the functional managers (group 1) had significantly higher scores than their staff members (group 2) on the Inspiration, Goal Setting, Problem

	FUNCTIONAL						PROJECT					
	MANAGER RANK ORDER			SUBORDINATE RANK ORDER			MANAGER RANK ORDER			SUBORDINATE RANK ORDER		
	NEED	BEH.	DIF.	NEED	BEH.	DIF.	NEED	BEH.	DIF.	NEED	BEH.	DIF.
1. Performance Emphasis	6	3	3	10	1	9	5	13	8	8	1	7
2. Consideration	19	13.5	5.5	14	13.5	.5	15.5	9	6.5	15	9.5	5.5
3. Inspiration	13	15	2	16	18.5	2.5	17.5	18	.5	13	17	4
4. Praise-Recognition	14	11.5	2.5	11	10.5	.5	11	9	2	10	17	7
5. Structuring Reward Contingencies	16	17	1	14	13.5	.5	11	13	2	11	12.5	1.5
6. Decision Participation	1	5.5	4.5	1	8.5	7.5	5	2.5	2.5	1.5	17	15.5
7. Autonomy-Delegation	3	3	0	2	4.5	2.5	8.5	2.5	6	3	5.5	2.5
8. Role Clarification	16	11.5	4.5	17.5	2.5	15	19	9	10	18	4	14
9. Goal Setting	2	8.5	6.5	4.5	4.5	0	8.5	5.5	3	8	2.5	5.5
10. Training-Coaching	11	18	7	12	16.5	4.5	13.5	16	2.5	16.5	7.5	9
11. Information Dissemination	9.5	8.5	1	6.5	13.5	7	5	2.5	2.5	4.5	9.5	5
12. Problem Solving	12	5.5	6.5	14	6.5	7.5	15.5	9	5.5	13	5.5	7.5
13. Planning	6	8.5	2.5	8.5	8.5	0	5	13	8	8	7.5	.5
14. Coordination	6	1	5	4.5	2.5	2	5	16	11	4.5	12.5	8
15. Work Facilitation	9.5	15	6.5	8.5	6.5	2	11	5.5	5.5	13	2.5	10.5
16. Representation	6	8.5	2.5	3	13.5	10.5	1.5	2.5	1	1.5	17	15.5
17. Interaction Facilitation	4	3	1	6.5	10.5	4	1.5	9	7.5	6	12.5	6.5
18. Conflict Management	18	15	3	19	16.5	2.5	17.5	16	1.5	19	12.5	6.5
19. Criticism-Discipline	16	19	3	17.5	18.5	1	13.5	19	5.5	16.5	17	.5

Table 3. Rank Orders for Mean Dimensional Need and Behavioral Skill Scores and Their Differences for Functional and Project Managers and Their Subordinates

Solving, Planning, and Conflict Management dimensions. Project managers (group 3) had significantly higher scores than their team members (group 4) on the Structuring Reward Contingencies dimension.

A comparison of functional managers and project managers (groups 1 and 3) indicated that functional managers' scores were significantly higher on the Coordination dimension.

Lastly, a comparison of functional staff members and project team members (groups 2 and 4) show that functional staff members had significantly higher scores on the Decision Participation, Autonomy-Delegation, Role Clarification, and Coordination dimensions, while project team members had a significantly higher score on the Training-Coaching dimension.

Both functional and project managers were again encouraged to share the results with their subordinates, especially on those dimensions where there were differences of one point or more. The scores for specific items comprising each dimension were provided to help the managers pinpoint differences between themselves and their staffs.

Areas Targeted for Management Development

Table 3 presents the rank orders of the mean need and behavior scores and the differences between the need and behavior ranks for each group. Each need-behavior dimension was placed in one of the three categories described earlier based on the differences between the need and behavior rankings. The criterion used was the mean difference of the rank differences for each group of managers and subordinates. This value was 3.5 for functional managers and 4.2 for their subordinates, and 4.8 for project managers and 6.9 for their subordinates.

Dimensions Requiring Decreases in Behavior Level

For functional managers, decreases in behavior were indicated if either the functional managers' need rank score was 3.5 or lower than the behavior rank score or if their subordinates' need rank score was 4.2 or lower than the behavior rank score. Table 3 shows that both functional managers and their subordinates reported that more emphasis than needed is placed on decision participation and training-coaching. Only functional managers perceived that more emphasis than necessary is placed on goal setting and work facilitation, while only their subordinates saw their managers as providing more information dissemination and representation than was needed.

Table 3 also provides the results for project managers and their team members. A dimension was placed in this category if either the project managers' need rank score was 4.8 or lower than their behavior rank score or if their team members' need rank score was 6.9 or lower than their behavior rank score.

Both project managers and their subordinates indicated the need for less coordination than each perceived project managers as exhibiting. Only project managers reported emphasizing more performance, planning, interaction-facilitation, and criticism discipline behaviors than they perceived were needed in the situation. On the other hand, only subordinates reported that their managers engaged in more praise-recognition, decision participation, and representation than they perceived the situation required.

Dimensions Requiring Increases in Skill Level

For functional managers and their subordinates, a dimension was placed in this category if either the functional managers' need rank score was 3.5 or higher than the behavior rank score or if their subordinates' need rank score was 4.2 or higher than the behavior rank score. Table 3 shows that both functional managers and their subordinates perceived need for more role- and problem-solving behavior than was presently being provided. Only functional managers reported a greater need for consideration and coordination, while only their subordinates reported a greater need for performance emphasis.

Increases in specific skills for project managers were indicated if the project managers' need rank score on a dimension was 4.8 or higher than the behavior rank score or if the team members' need rank score was 6.9 or higher than the behavior rank score. Both project managers and their subordinates reported a need for more role clarification, problem solving, and work facilitation. Only project managers perceived a need for more consideration and autonomy-delegation, and only their subordinates reported the need for more performance emphasis, goal setting, and training-coaching.

Dimensions Requiring No Change in Behavior Level

For functional managers, a dimension was placed in this category if the difference between the functional managers' need and behavior rank score was less than 3.5 and if the difference between their subordinates' need and behavior rank score was less than 4.2. Table 3 shows that the behavior dimensions of Inspiration, Praise-Recognition, Structuring Reward Contingencies, Autonomy-Delegation, Planning, Interaction Facilitation, Conflict Management, and Criticism-Discipline appeared to be appropriately suited to the situation.

For project managers, no training was required in a dimension when the difference between the project managers' need and behavior rank score was less than 4.8, and the difference between team members' need and behavior rank score was less than 6.9. As shown in Table 3, project managers appear to have appropriate skills in the dimensions of Inspiration, Structuring Reward Contingencies, Goal Setting, Information Dissemination, and Conflict Management.

Conclusion

The results of this study show the importance of a situational approach to the management development of project and functional managers. Behavioral recommendations from theory and research may provide some general guidelines for these managers to follow, but the current results indicate that the most appropriate choice of behaviors depends on the leadership situation. For example, the finding in this study that both project and functional managers and their subordinates perceived the need for more role clarification and problem solving is consistent with previous research in the area of matrix leadership. However, it is also generally presumed that participation in decision-making is critical to effective leadership in matrix organizations. In this study, subordinates of both project and functional managers felt that their managers were placing more emphasis on decision participation than was required by the situation.

The results of the application of this approach also demonstrated the need to use the inputs of both supervisors and their subordinates in designing and implementing a management development training effort. All too often, the effectiveness of such a program is less than it should be because the inputs of subordinates were not sought or considered. This study showed that, in many instances, subordinates were seeking specific actions from their managers, while managers were concentrating on other areas. For example, subordinates of project managers wanted their leaders to engage in more task-oriented behaviors, e.g., performance emphasis, goal setting, and training-coaching. On the other hand, project managers themselves felt that the situation called for more relationship-oriented behaviors, e.g., consideration and autonomy-delegation. Similarly, functional managers perceived that more emphasis on consideration and coordination was needed, while subordinates were looking for more performance emphasis. Discovering these differences in perception and determining their cause is the first big step in developing an effective training program.

Programs such as the one reported here will be essential to the development of skills needed to manage in the unique situation of the project and functional manager. Such an approach not only provides more accurate information regarding areas in which training and development are needed, but it also ensures that all parties will be receptive to the subsequent development effort.

References

1. Dilworth, J.B., R.C. Ford, P.M. Ginter, and A.C. Rucks. 1985. Centralized Project Management. *Journal of Systems Management* (August): 30–35.

2. Dressler, D.M. 1986. In Project Management, the Emphasis Should Be on Management. *Data Management* (January): 62.

3. Joyce, W. F. Matrix Organization: A Social Experiment. *Academy of Management Journal* 29, no. 3: 536–561.

4. Katz, R., and T.J. Allen. 1985. Project Performance and the Locus of Influence in the R&D Matrix. *Academy of Management Journal* 28, no. 1: 67–87.

5. Kerzner, H. 1981. The R&D Project Manager. *Project Management Quarterly* (June): 20–24.

6. Phillips, R.C. 1985. Project Conflict: Cost, Causes, and Cures. *Public Utilities Fortnightly* (May 16): 35–39.

7. Salinger, A.W. 1985. Leadership, Communication Skills Lift Projects to Success. *Data Management* (September): 36–37.

8. Yukl, G.A. 1981. *Leadership in Organizations.* Englewood Cliffs, N.J.: Prentice Hall, Inc.

The Project Manager as Team Builder: Creating an Effective Team

Lawrence Todryk, P.E., MS, MBA, Adjunct Professor, DeVry Institute of Technology

Project Management Journal 21, no. 4 (December 1990)

T HE DESIGN AND construction of small to large projects presents a unique set of opportunities for the project manager to learn how to manage projects more effectively. Dr. Dave Cleland, researcher and educator, has brought home the consequences of poor leadership and lack of clarity in the organizational design of a project team (3).

A close look at NASA's Challenger Program brings to light some critical issues. When organizational design is not clear, leadership not defined, and teams do not work together effectively, detrimental consequences will result. *Fortune* magazine noted that the flow of information up and down the NASA hierarchy was as flawed as the notorious O-rings themselves. Instead of working together and communicating, the Johnson, Kennedy, and Marshall Space Centers behaved more like chiefdoms and did not work together with NASA management (2).

The Public Utility Commission of New York recommended an exclusion from the rate base. They noted a $1.2 billion overrun being improperly applied to the project cost. The overrun was due to poor organizational design, which lacked clarity, authority, and project responsibility (8).

Another significant example is the track record of the TVA. The TVA expended in excess of $15 billion on the construction of nine nuclear power plants, and not one is successfully operating. The plants have been delayed by schedule, safety, and operations problems. *Fortune* magazine noted that the TVA has been handicapped by a lack of strong leadership with nuclear power experience. Lack of clarity and weak leadership has led to departmental infighting (4).

Cost overruns and scheduling delays posed major problems to the management team constructing Chicago's McCormick Place. Governor Thompson called in a special team to address the cost overruns and place the construction back on schedule.

Today, project managers face an increase in the number of variables they address, thus increasing the probability of cost overruns, delayed schedules, and poor project authority and leadership. Projects such as nuclear power plants and deep tunnel construction are facing increasing scrutiny for accident rates and fatalities. A weak management team usually leads to poor quality construction that fails to pass quality control tests, requires reconstruction, delays the schedule, and increases the project cost. All levels of a project manager's work environment are in a dynamic state. Cyclical and structural changes that occur in the economy and society also have impact on the project manager's work environment. The project manager has to function within markets that are affected by economic cycles of expansion and recession and structural changes in society that are occurring more rapidly than ever before.

Leon Martel, in his address to PMI International in 1986, stated that the computer industry is an example of rapid technological change. He noted that both IBM and Japan have recently developed a computer chip capable of storing one million bytes of information, with a four-million-byte chip to be brought to market in 1991. This implies that the operational storage capacity of a mainframe computer could be placed inside a device the size of the original hand-held calculator. These changes will mean increased opportunities for the project manager to respond to those structural changes in ways that support her organization's mission.

Cost overruns and poor production in the construction industry wastes an estimated $10 billion per year. A result of this waste is an increase in the cost of energy, transportation, and consumer services. The author proposes that the implementation of an effective team-building process, in a project management environment, will measurably reduce schedule delays and cost overruns while improving the quality of team morale and increasing productivity. The team-building skills and concepts presented in the remainder of this article are tools that the project manager may implement in developing the project team.

Tools for the Project Manager

Change has a noticeable impact on team productivity and effectiveness. The project manager's ability to create an effective team is essential in responding to accelerated changes in technology, social attitudes, and human values.

Buchollz states that the team and organizational culture—the ideas, customs, skills, arts, and values of a team—impact team productivity, effectiveness and profitability (1). One way of addressing the question of culture is to recognize that a team culture exists whether the culture is or isn't addressed. The values, attitudes, skills, and ideas of the team can be positively influenced by the project manager. The manager's behavior sets the group culture. Lee Iacocca said, "The speed of the boss is the speed of the team."

Most team members recognize that paying keen attention to what the manager does and less to what the manager says is the best way to get ahead in the organization. The value system and belief system of the manager is usually mirrored by the members' actions, values, and attitudes; therefore, a work culture should be purposefully created. If ignored, the environment outside the project team will create the team culture. This often results in undesirable delays in schedule, cost overruns, increases in accident rates, and additional rework.

One method of improving the nature and quality of the team is to have a clear mission statement. A sample mission statement is: "This team exists to: design, construct, and place into successful service a new parking facility that effectively meets the needs of the client." Another way of saying it is, "What are we here to do?" It is essential that each team member answer that question in the same manner. Lack of clarity and agreement in the mission of the project leads to conflicts, cost overruns, and exceeded budgets.

Ernest Tolle of IBM presents an effective framework for the development of mission statements (7). The mission statement should include a specific description of who, what, when, and the relationship to the client of the project. The elements for project mission criteria are:

Purpose. State the reason the project exists and its major activities.

Uniqueness. The statement should include the uniqueness in skills and tasks the team provides in relationship to the client.

Semantically Unambiguous. Words that describe precisely with a common content are used to write the mission statement.

Succinctness. Brevity is the object with accuracy and completeness for ease in remembering and use.

Pre- and Proscribed Activities. With clarity in the mission statement, the team's limits become clear.

Reasonably Stable. The mission should be constant and not change with every minor shift in the project.

Supports Higher Level Mission. The project mission supports the higher mission of the project team's client organization. This includes the client and the project team organizations. If there are consultants on the team, each organization's mission needs to support the others.

A strong mission statement calls the members of the project team into action and creates a natural framework to generate goals and schedules. Generating a project team mission statement formed by group process is an effective tool in the team-building process. It is essential for the project manager to keep the mission up-front and visible by action and in writing. The actions of the manager must reflect the mission of the team. The project manager's actions must reflect the desired team culture. If a project manager expects the team culture and mission to be integrated in the actions and values of the team members, example is the most effective manner to produce this result. When a manager exhibits values and attitudes that are incongruent with the stated team mission and culture, the results usually will be conflicting. The author proposes that significant project failures, such as those described in the introduction, probably had a poorly developed mission statement. The team members probably were not aware of the project's mission and how their work supported the project.

To generate a performance-based work culture, team members need to expand existing skills and master new ones. The project manager needs to be supportive of team members who are willing to learn new skills, attitudes, methods, and procedures so that the team can be more effective and obtain team goals. This is an essential component in developing a supportive work culture that is responsive to accelerated changes on project teams.

How does the project manager support the learning and growth of new skills and attitudes? Some effective ways include:

- Defining in detail the skills and attitudes to be learned, including time frames and expected results. This provides clarity and accountability for the learning process.
- Holding regular feedback and support sessions to review the learning contract. Offering feedback, constructive advice, and recognition for jobs well done is essential. Recognition by the project manager is a strong and important tool in providing motivation to continue learning new skills and attitudes.

Characteristics of an Effective Team

What are the characteristics of an effective work team, and how does the project manager develop it? Dave Francis and Don Young are consultants and researchers in the field of team building. They have developed a model that describes the characteristics of an effective team. The appendix is a synopsis of the model (5). The following is a summary of the author's evaluation and comments on this model.

Appropriate Leadership

The single most important factor in establishing and maintaining quality work and effective teamwork is leadership. Diverse and long-term projects demand that the project manager have a variety of usable leadership styles to meet the challenges of management. Generally, the project manager with the widest range of leadership skills and the ability to use them is most effective.

Young and Francis state that clarifying objectives and working through relevant issues provides a natural means of team development (5). Team members learn new skills and attitudes and improve team effectiveness by exploring and addressing the issues that affect them. Differences between team members and project team issues can become a source of strength for the team if dealt with in an open and effective problem-solving manner.

Suitable Team Membership

You can't turn a herd of turtles into a twenty-mule work team. This is another way of saying that it is usually a management risk to recruit someone who does not have the basic technical and management skills required to successfully perform in a team. When designing or compiling a team, it is important to recognize that a team is more than the summation of all the skills and attitudes of its members. In an effective team there is a synergy and esprit de corps that is created that will address the challenges of the team.

Team Commitment

The degree of commitment shown by a precision drum and bugle corp is obviously different from a group of college freshman playing intramural basketball. The precision, accuracy, and effectiveness of a work team that shows a high degree of commitment is exciting and energizing to observe. It's similar to the speed and accuracy of a racing pit team for the Indy 500. They change four tires, fuel up, and check all the critical points on the engine within twelve seconds. This requires discipline, commitment, and a high degree of team effort. Committed team members value the contributions of the other members and usually express their feelings and concerns openly. This kind of cooperation enhances mutual respect among team members. Consistent feedback on individual performance enhances team commitment. Sometimes negative feedback can be used successfully to maintain team commitment, as well as encouragement that acknowledges a job well done.

Team Climate

The informal rules, values, and attitudes established in the course of team development can affect end results as well as moment-to-moment interaction. It is the responsibility of the project manager to establish the customs, culture, and values of the team. These values should generate a positive team climate. Team building requires an openness to establish relationships that are genuine, honest, and supportive of change. Francis and Young emphasize that it should be possible for team members to be wrong without being made to feel foolish or admonished (5). A NASA chief has noted that "We do not punish error, we only punish the suppression of error." Some of the advantages of openness are:
- More honest and supportive relationships
- Problems and issues clarified and dealt with
- An increase in creativity and problem-solving ability
- Greater clarity in communication and working results
- Negative effects of bureaucracy are reduced.
  Some potential concerns in group openness are:
- Communication becomes more specific in feedback to management and all team members, requiring individuals to deal with vulnerability.

- Ignored problems come to the surface.
- Some members may feel threatened and become hostile in their reactions.

Team Achievement

Effective team achievement is based on the clarity of goals, team purpose, and the team's ability to deliver specific goals. An effective team sets high standards of achievement. In order to consistently maintain team performance, achievements/goals should be acknowledged and rewarded.

Clear Roles within Corporation/Agency

The project team's function and purpose within a corporation or an agency needs to be clear. Reports and oral communication between the team and other corporate divisions should reinforce and support the team's identity within the corporation or agency. It is essential that the project executive maintain a strong degree of clarity and not compromise the project mission when communicating with project stakeholders.

Effective Work Methods and Procedures

Work methods are tools with which the work is performed. Procedures relate to how the work is performed and its flow. The design and implementation of these two elements are necessary for the team to be effective. In the project environment, the author recommends that the team have input into the design of work method tools. Due to the uniqueness of the project environment, it is critical that the work methods be effective in meeting the needs of the entire project team.

Team Organization

Team organization is the primary responsibility of the project manager. Role definition, clarity of communication, an operational plan, and agreement on purpose creates a context for a highly effective team organization. As stated previously, if team organization is ignored, successful team development can be significantly impeded. The top leadership of the project team needs to design and communicate these parameters to the project stakeholders.

Critiquing without Rancor

When the team is not producing the desired results, direct feedback is vital for course correction. If all members are able to give and receive feedback, relationships will be clear, and self-critiquing facilitates team evolvement. Feedback stated effectively can be an invitation to change. Stated inappropriately, feedback can result in a retreat back to old secure behaviors.

Individual Development

A team is effective to the degree that it can harness the strengths of the individual and align them behind the mission of the team. According to Francis and Young, the qualities of a strongly developed individual includes:
- High energy
- In touch with feelings
- Open to taking risks
- Willingness to be flexible
- Willingness to openly communicate.

Creative Capacity

Creative abilities are nurtured by open communication between all team members. A lack of communication often blocks creativity. Addressing these blocks is an effective way to enhance creativity. This responsibility also falls on the project manager. Here, a group facilitation process may be used to improve creativity.

Inter-Group Relationships

Inter-group relationship is the ability of each member to communicate and support each other while working on a project team. There is a direct correlation between inter-group relationships and the successful achievement of the team purpose and goals. Strong relationships achieve goals more effectively.

How Does a Project Manager Become a Team Builder?

Implementing a team-building process requires a different set of skills than normally utilized by the project manager in managing project teams. An understanding of human relationship skills and group dynamics is necessary to implement change.

A project manager who walks into a senior manager's office and states a desire to implement a process for change may get a strong negative response. The project manager must present his ideas in a manner that convinces senior management to support the team-building process. The project manager should regularly apprise management of the team's progress and communicate any anticipated needs. The support of senior management helps to ensure the completion of the project's goals.

The project manager is responsible for the development of the team. There are two basic ways for a project manager to learn team-building skills:

1. Participate in a hands-on team-building seminar.

2. Bring in a team-building consultant to design and implement a team procedure to meet the specific needs of your team in your organization.

Making the appropriate choice requires the project manager to observe her own personal strengths and the strengths of the organization and project team.

When should a project manager decide to use a consultant for team development? Perhaps it is better to list some of the services a consultant would provide. The consultant would help the project manager:

- Start up a team development process and train a project manager in team development.
- Address controversy and sensitive issues.
- Give objective feedback on team performance and work procedures.
- Give support to changing behaviors, attitudes, and support group goals.
- Manage and take part in generating the team development process when project team managers and members are lacking in the skills and time.

Francis and Young note some of the areas in which the team-building consultant can help the team. They are:

- Identifying and assessing blockages to effective team working
- Identifying, confronting, and resolving the problems with the team
- Assisting in establishing team development objectives and charting their progress (5).

Stages of Team Development

The team-building process has defined stages that a team goes through from inception (compiling-creating) to mature and effective working relationships. This is especially true in project management environments where you direct a number of project teams functioning on the same project. Each project team has its own purpose, schedule, and budget of resources. Multiproject examples would be the large design and construction programs, such as the renovation of O'Hare International Airport, which had in excess of 100 project teams; the Milwaukee Metropolitan Sewage Commission design and renovation of its treatment and collection facilities; and the design and construction of nuclear power plants. Art Freedman, Ph.D., has noted the importance of transition management during construction and after completion of a major operating facility. The coordination and the interrelationships between project teams during design and construction is of major importance to assure the successful completion of the project on schedule and within budget. When different project teams handle various levels of a project, whether it's in the construction industry or the corporate environment, transition and project management is necessary.

At any given time, each individual project team will be at its own stage of development. The overall project team will also have its own stage of development. One of the easiest models to understand and utilize for stages of team development was developed by Francis and Young and is called Stages of Team Development (5).

Stage One: Testing

The team members react in their own manner to the challenge of meeting new colleagues. Team members present themselves in their own ways; some may be fearful, outgoing, controlling, or reserved. At this stage, team members may appear to be acting effectively, progressing with their tasks and generating what may appear to be harmonious and effective working relationships. This is usually only skin deep because the initial effectiveness comes from attitudes and training established prior to the team being formed.

Stage Two: Infighting

As the team develops, it becomes necessary to sort out personal relationships of power and influence. Individual alliances are formed, and people emerge as particularly significant. Team members will observe and evaluate the team member's behavior. They may accept his leadership, or they may find cunning ways to avoid it. During this stage, teams decide how they are going to operate. Generally this is done by subterranean (covert) communication with little or no explicit planning. In essence, all the issues are concerned with control; the three questions that dominate are:
1. Who controls the team?
2. How is control exercised?
3. What happens to delinquents?

The team has to find the answer to these questions before the next stage of development can occur. Covert issues and difficulties must be confronted or evaded. Some teams never make it to the next stage due to a lack of addressing the control issues.

Stage Three: Getting Organized

Following the successful resolution of the issues surrounding control, the team begins to tackle its work with a new energy. Team members will tend to work together and have committed themselves to making the team work. This is an important stage because the team needs the support and interest of all team members. Without this, individual preoccupations will tend to dominate, and the team will tend to fail to grow.

The work team becomes identified with the precision and contribution being made by the team members, and their contributions are discussed and measured. Typically the quality of listening improves, and members begin to respect each other's contributions. Team members become more concerned with the economy of effort and task effectiveness. At this stage, the team has to grow in its capacity to handle problems effectively. Without this evolution of working methods the team will continue using barely effective modes of operation, satisfying itself with adequate effectiveness rather than striving for excellence.

Stage Four: Mature Closeness

The team members of a fully developed team form a rapport and closeness. Sometimes this is so strong that long-term bonds are forged. Team members are prepared to extend themselves for their colleagues, and real enjoyment of each other is typical. A mature team has taken definite steps to clarify the team's organization to improve work methods and increase team effectiveness.

The model of the stages of team development provides a framework for the project manager to access and generate a course correction if a team is not developing correctly. The process of team development provides a strong set of resources for the project manager to utilize in managing teams that are effectively meeting the project goals and schedule.

The Benefits and Rewards of Team Building

The benefits and rewards of team building are numerous. Some of the benefits I have observed are:
- Increased ability to respond to project needs
- Rapid and accurate response to needs
- Highly motivated teams that provide a means for team members to make a viable contribution
- Increased quality of work and decisions
- Increased collective team strength resulting in a greater ability to complete projects on time
- Team members committed to increasing their personal effectiveness, thereby improving collective team ability.

I propose that if team-building procedures are implemented, whether on construction programs or within the corporate environment, the effectiveness of the project team will increase. This will result in reduced project costs, accident rates, hiring and training costs, redoing of contract work, and improved quality of project work.

Addressing the Cycles of Change

Project managers are continuously addressing the necessity to implement change. Change, according to Leon Martel, occurs in cycles or as a major structural change, which is non-reversible (6). Examples of cyclical change are fluctuations in interest rates and stock prices, changes in centralization versus decentralization of large corporations, and the available supply of professionals. The cycle of project funding is a condition that directly influences the project manager's ability to manage projects. Structural changes include changes in new technology, such as the use of personal computers, and the integration of women into the work force.

Importance of	a – Most	b – Highly	c – Less
1 – Most	1a	1b	1c
2 – Moderately	2a	2b	2c
3 – Less	3a	3b	3c

Figure 1   Matrix Analysis of Change

Leon Martel recommends certain key elements be integrated into a strategy for mastering change. The following is a summary of these elements (6).
- Recognize that change is occurring. Even if things seem to be in a state of consistency, change will occur. The cycle may be longer than previously observed.
- Identify the changes that are likely to affect one's particular project and professional and personal life.
- Determine the type and probable pattern of each identified change.
- Rank the changes by the importance level of their effect and the likelihood of their occurrences.
- Make use of the changes in implementing a strategy for successful completion of your project.

Refering to Figure 1, Matrix Analysis of Change, obviously the 1a, 1b, 2a, and 2b issues are the areas that are the most critical for a project manager to address. Changes in 3a, 3b, and 3c do not deserve immediate attention.

Recognizing patterns of change and mastering response strategies enable the project manager to develop different modes of action that support the purpose of the project. Team building is a dynamic ongoing process that facilitates change within the work team. The strategy Leon Martel is suggesting is a natural set of tools that can easily be integrated into the team-building process. This integration will greatly improve the effectiveness of the team-building effort and the ability of the project team to obtain its goals and schedules.

Summary and Conclusion

The project management environment is in a continual state of both cyclical and structural change, which results in significant delays in schedules, cost overruns, accident rate increases, and redoing of contract work. The described team-building procedures and processes offer efficient possibilities to the project manager for creating a more effective team. It is proposed that the implementation of an effective team-building process in a project management environment will measurably reduce schedule delays and cost overruns, improve the quality of work and team morale, and increase the productivity and skill level of the team. It is highly recommended that the project manager acquire team-building skills to increase the project team's effectiveness.

References

1. Buchollz, Steve. 1985. *The Positive Manager.* New York: Wiley & Sons.

2. Brody, Michael. 1986. NASA's Challenge: Ending Isolation at the Top. *Fortune* (May 12).

3. Cleland, Dave. 1987. Prudent Project Organizational Design. Paper Presentation, International Symposium (October 7): 159–166.

4. Dumain, Brian. 1986. Nuclear Scandal Shakes the TVA. *Fortune* (October 27): 41.

5. Francis, Dave, and Don Young. *Improving Work Groups; A Practical Manual for Team Building.* California: University Associates, Inc.

6. Martel, Leon. 1986. *Mastering Change.* New York: Simon & Schuster.

7. Tolle Jr., Ernest. 1988. Developing the Mission Statement; Why, When and How. *Organizational Development Journal* 16, no. 1 (Spring): 15.

8. Restatement from the Recommended Decision by Administrative Law Judges, C. Levey and Thomas N. Matias, March 13, 1985, Case No. 27563. *Long Island Lighting Company-Shoreham Providence Investigation, State of New York, Public Service Commission.*

Appendix: Characteristics of an Effective Team

A team that is mature and effective has been painstakingly built. Problems have been worked through, relationships deepened, and roles clarified. When successful teams are examined, we find that they have achieved definite progress in the following areas.

Appropriate Leadership. The team manager has the skills and the intention to develop a team approach and allocates time to team-building activities. Management in the team is seen as a shared function. Individuals other than the manager are given the opportunity to exercise leadership when their skills are appropriate to the needs of the team.

Suitable Membership. Team members are individually qualified and capable of contributing the mix of skills and characteristics that provide an appropriate balance.

Commitment to the Team. Team members feel a sense of individual commitment to the aims and purposes of the team. They are willing to devote personal energy to building the team and supporting other team members. When working outside the team boundaries, the members feel a sense of belonging to and representing the team.

Constructive Climate. The team has developed a climate in which people feel relaxed, able to be direct and open, and prepared to take risks.

Concern to Achieve. The team is clear about its objectives, which are felt to be worthwhile. It sets targets of performance that are felt to be stretching but achievable. Energy is mainly devoted to the achievement of results, and team performance is reviewed frequently to see where improvements can be made.

Clear Department Role. The team has contributed to department planning and has a distinct and productive role within the overall organization.

Effective Work Methods. The team has developed lively, systematic, and effective ways to solve problems together.

Well-Organized Team Procedures. Roles are clearly defined, communication patterns are well developed, and administrative procedures support a team approach.

Critique without Rancor. Team and individual errors and weaknesses are examined, without personal attack, to enable the group to learn from its experiences.

Well-Developed Individuals. Team members are deliberately developed, and the team can cope with strong individual contributions.

Creative Strength. The team has the capacity to create new ideas through the interactions of its members. Some innovative risk taking is rewarded, and the team will support new ideas from individual members or from outside. Good ideas are followed through into action.

Positive Inter-Group Relations. Relationships with other teams have been systematically developed to provide open personal contact and identify when joint working may give maximum payoff. There is regular contact and review of joint or collective priorities with other teams. Individuals are encouraged to contact and work with members of other teams.

Design of Project Management Systems from Top Management's Perspective

Christian Navarre, Faculty of Administration, University of Ottawa,
Ottawa, Ontario, Canada
Jean-Louis Schaan, Faculty of Administration, University of Ottawa,
Ottawa, Ontario, Canada

Project Management Journal 21, no. 2 (June 1990)

THE LONG-TERM SURVIVAL of any organization is in part dependent on management's ability to develop and implement corporate strategies in tune with its ever-changing environments (2) (6) (10) (12) (14). Generally, the strategic "fine-tuning" between an organization and its environment is effected through projects such as investments, new products, internal reorganization, and so on. A major challenge for top managers is to institutionalize a process of constant organizational renewal through the implementation of project management methods that will maximize the proportion of successful projects under increasingly severe resource constraints. Meeting this challenge implies paying attention to project-related activities such as the generation of an ongoing stream of new project ideas, screening of project proposals, allocation of resources to projects, execution and control of projects, and so on (2) (3) (4) (12).

Project management (15) (18) refers to the methods and techniques created for the conception, analysis, and implementation of temporary work efforts—highly irreversible and non-repetitive—under time constraints and with limited and scarce resources (14). Project management integrates these activities, in a coherent fashion, to guide an idea from its conceptual phase to its successful execution. Project management (1) (8) (9) (11) (13) (17) (20) is defined in a broad sense and applies equally to construction of a hospital, development of a new product, or production of a play or a film. This definition is consistent with the Project Management Institute's definition (see *A Guide to the Project Management Body of Knowledge [PMBOK Guide]*).

At least three reasons may explain why, in an increasingly competitive and volatile environment, projects are of growing strategic importance to the renewal and survival of any organization (4) (11) (19).

First, the timing and successful implementation of projects can greatly enhance an organization's competitive situation. For instance, the reduction of the time required to bring a new product to market can contribute to the erection of barriers to entry for others, altering the dynamics of competition, and, in the end, determining the overall profitability of the project. Time, in general, and speed of execution, in particular, have long been considered constraints in making strategic decisions. Today they are increasingly considered a strategic factor that needs to be managed as any other resource.

Second, projects are net consumers of an organization's resources such as cash flow, people, and equipment. As such, projects only produce a return when successfully implemented. The goal of any project management system is to transfer projects into stable operations that will eventually generate liquidity (5) (6). However, there is always a consumption of resources that inevitably lowers the organization's financial mobility, at least temporarily. In such circumstances, only a superior authority can legitimate the transfers of resources and assume the associated risks. The expectation of senior managers is that projects become stable operations, a necessary condition to the recovery of the capital invested and to the release of profitability.

Third, projects can involve significant changes to the infrastructure of an organization. Projects often require the destabilization of the existing order (7) (21) when they necessitate the destruction and restructuring of the internal workings of the organization. Projects are a source of deviation. They create tension and provoke the emergence of micro-cultures. Thus, project implementation calls for skilled top management commitment and leadership, as well as for the existence and protection of project champions.

Following brief comments on the sources of data that led to this article, an overview of the major managerial implications associated with the management of a project, as compared with the management of a portfolio of projects, is provided. The article then identifies important project characteristics in the determination of appropriate management practices. Finally, it concludes with the identification of key roles performed by top managers in relation to projects.

Methodological Observations

This article is based on two field studies:

1. The analysis of interviews conducted with forty-four senior executives in thirty-four organizations; the following summarizes some of the characteristics of these organizations:

- The sample was comprised of ten manufacturing firms, sixteen engineering firms, four government organizations, three start-up firms, and one in the banking sector.
- Twenty-eight were medium-to-large organizations; six were small.
- Seventeen organizations operated under well-established project management procedures; seven were undergoing major modifications to their project management practices; and in eight organizations managers indicated that their project management systems were in a state of crisis.
- Twenty organizations operated with a single project management system while eleven operated with several systems simultaneously.
- The dominant project management structure was matrix (eighteen organizations), followed by a project-based structure (eleven organizations).

2. A survey conducted among the chief executive officers of the one hundred largest Canadian organizations; a sample interview and sample survey questions are presented in the appendix.

- Twenty-seven of the thirty-three firms responding had operating budgets of $100 million or more. Sixty-five percent of the respondents were at the president or vice president level.
- Managers appear to have the greatest difficulties with projects that have high uncertainty with regard to the technology they involve. On average, the managers in the organizations that faced low market uncertainty and high technology uncertainty rated the effectiveness of their project management methods at 57.50 percent. The managers in the organizations that faced low market uncertainty and low technology uncertainty rated their effectiveness at 77.08 percent, and those facing high market uncertainty and low technology uncertainty rated their effectiveness at 76.33 percent.
- The organizations surveyed had considerable experience with projects. Each organization managed an average of 230 projects at any one time. Some were continuously busy with one hundred projects, while others could supervise up to four hundred projects at the same time. Altogether, the thirty-three organizations undertook over four thousand projects.
- All organizations had a project portfolio profile that included a multitude of small projects and a few larger ones. The budget of the project portfolio did not represent more than 15 percent of any organization's total operating budget.

Project Management versus Project Portfolio Management

Except in the case of small enterprises, top executives seldom functioned as project managers. In fact, the smaller projects in an organization seldom reached the attention of the higher levels of the hierarchy. Hence, the concept of project management does not carry the same meaning for a project manager as for a manager of project managers.

The fundamental distinction between a project manager and a manager of project managers stems from the difference in orientation between the two levels of managers. Top managers are responsible for the successful management of their organizations' operations and, at the same time, of several projects, all at different stages of development, facing different levels of uncertainty and ambiguity, and involving different levels of complexity. On the other hand, a project manager is the individual responsible for the success of a specific project. Hence, top managers manage a portfolio of projects. Portfolio project management is of a higher order of magnitude than project management (see Table 1).

Preoccupations differ in the following areas:

Organizational Level. In the organizations we surveyed, vice presidents and division managers played the pivotal roles with respect to project management practices. They are the key players at the top management level.

Key Goals. A fundamental concern at the top management level is the renewal of the overall portfolio of projects. Senior executives are interested in maximizing the profitability of each project separately but, more importantly, they also are interested in maximizing the proportion of projects brought to a successful completion. At the project level, success is measured on the basis of time, monetary cost, and project performance.

Staffing. Top level managers are generally involved in the selection of the project manager who, in turn, will be responsible for the selection of the project team.

Planning Tasks. The results from our survey indicate that, in general, top managers limit their involvement to the definition of a project's objectives, its broad articulation, and the control of the trajectory. The project manager, on the other hand, is responsible for the detailed planning and the design of a built-in evaluation system for the project.

Time Orientation. Project management is considered a permanent activity for top managers for whom the constant renewal of the project portfolio is a vital ingredient to the long-term survival and growth of the organization. The time horizon for a project manager, on the other hand, is dictated by the expected completion date of the project for which the manager is responsible.

Resource Allocation. Top managers are primarily interested in allocating limited resources among competing demands from operational and project activities. Resources are not allocated to a specific project on the basis of its merits alone but rather in relation to other opportunities for maximizing the long-term return on those resources for the organization as a whole. Breaking down a project portfolio into the following elements helps put in perspective some of the tradeoffs that senior managers need to make when managing and allocating resources to a portfolio of projects:

	Portfolio of Projects	**Single Project**
Organizational Level	Vice-presidents Division general managers	Project manager
Key Goals	Overall performance of the project's portfolio	Time, cost, quality
Staffing	Selection of project managers by top level managers	Selection of the project team by the project manager
Planning Tasks	Global formulation of project goals and objectives Overall planning and control	Detailed formulation of project goals and objectives Continuous planning and control of the project
Time Orientation	Long-term: Permanent management of constant flow of temporary activities	Short-term: Management of temporary activities
Resource Allocation	Allocation of limited resources within a portfolio to maximize its long-term return	Efficient and effective allocation of resources to the project
Conflict Resolution	Resolution of conflicts between projects	Resolution of conflicts within a project

Table 1 Determining Factors in Project Management: The Management of a Project's Portfolio versus the Management of a Single Project

$$P = \{p\}^o - \{p\}^c - \{p\}^f - \{p\}^s + \{p\}^n$$

P = portfolio of projects

p^o = **ongoing projects**

p^c = **completed projects**

p^f = **failed projects**

p^s = **shelved projects**

p^n = **new projects**

On the other hand, a project manager's primary concern is with the efficiency and effectiveness with which a project's resources are allocated to predetermined project tasks.

Conflict Resolution. Top managers are frequently involved in resolving conflicts and tradeoffs between projects of a given portfolio, while project managers are required to resolve conflicts within a given project.

Thus, project portfolio management places top management in a unique perspective with respect to project management and one that is different from that of project managers. What then is the nature of top management involvement with project management practices in its organizations?

Key Top Management Tasks and Roles

During our interviews, we discovered that top managers were involved in one or several of a limited number of areas related to project managers. These are:

Definition of General Philosophy. In defining an organization's goals, objectives, and strategic orientation, top management sends signals expressing its expectations and priorities. These signals indicate the kinds of products, markets, and technologies that the organization intends to emphasize in the future and, hence, the kinds of projects that are deemed desirable to support the successful execution of the strategy. The institutionalization of such objectives and priorities is further reinforced by organizational arrangements such as the planning process, the resource allocation process, performance measurement systems, promotion systems ("You won't get ahead if you do not come up with good project ideas"), and so on. In some companies, top management clearly makes a strategic decision when it decides the proportion of funds to be allocated to offensive versus maintenance or replacement projects. Thus, top management influences the number and the kinds of projects initiated and undertaken.

Top management can play a key role in influencing the actual management of projects by defining elements of the project management philosophy. The data suggest two manners in which this can be done: top management may establish basic project principles to which all managers need to conform, or, in the case of very large projects, it may define the specific approach to contracting for a project.

In a limited number of organizations, top managers tried to encourage their people to initiate project ideas. These top managers considered the infusion of their organizations' cultures with a project mentality an important responsibility.

Selection of Key People. Top management may want to assign or approve the key players in project activities including project managers, partners, negotiating team members, or consultants. Even in firms relying to a large extent on outside expertise, top management assigned the project management function to an insider who represented the owner, someone who was familiar with the organization, and who knew where and how to obtain information and approvals. This attitude was justified by the desire to improve effectiveness and maintain some level of control. On the one hand, it was clear that learning those skills and understanding the organization would be too costly and time-consuming for an outsider. On the other hand, in a world where managers resort more and more to strategic alliances and contractual relationships of all sorts, this was seen as an effective way to keep some measure of control over projects.

Screening and Selection of Projects. Although clearly of importance, no general patterns of top management involvement emerged here. In some cases, a project required the concurrence of all functional areas of the organization (personnel, finance, marketing, production, and so on), while in other cases only relevant people were consulted. In still other cases, the number of inputs was kept to a minimum in order to avoid unrealistic specifications. For manufacturing firms, early screening was based on strategic fit and preliminary financial projections, which in turn determined whether an in-depth feasibility study was justified or not.

The collective experience of the managers interviewed suggests that the probability of success of a given project is most likely when:

- The screening methods are selective and severe; screening is effected through a formalized administrative process.
- The number of projects subjected to the screening procedure is high, and the projects are of great diversity. The overall size and quality of the initial project base depends to a large extent on the collective and individual creativity of the people employed by the organization.
- The portfolio of projects engaged in subsequent phases is small enough that it does not unduly tax the organization's managerial capability.

Resource Allocation. Key resources can be allocated in two ways:

- Directly to a project or
- Through an envelope formula.

If the envelope formula is selected, it is up to the manager who receives the envelope to decide how it should be allocated among ongoing operations and projects first, and then among projects.

Whatever the approach, it is essential that the process be clear and perceived to be fair by the organization. The latter is achieved by either specifying the criteria and the process through which projects are going to be prioritized or by setting mechanisms for appealing resource allocation decisions.

An important mechanism in shaping future project proposals is the capital appropriation request. This permits top management to shape the kinds of projects that are eventually submitted, as managers learn over time which projects are supported, and to what extent, and which are not supported at all.

Support to Project Activities. Another key concern for top managers is to stabilize the flow of resources allocated to projects once the latter are under way. One firm, operating in a highly cyclical industry, had implemented an interesting concept to shelter its projects from the impact of fluctuations in cash flows. Its strategy was to select four major projects at any given time, with the understanding that three projects would be fully funded while the fourth one, the swing-project, would absorb the fluctuations. This can be very frustrating for the swing-project manager who needs to continuously adjust his schedule. But once one of the other projects is completed, the swing-project becomes a priority and is part of the three regular projects. A new project is then assigned the status of swing-project.

In addition to showing their commitment and interest for ongoing projects, senior executives considered it important to promote cooperation between groups on different projects. Their objective was to see cooperation take place without their having to resort to rules or sanctions.

Management of Transitions in Project Phases. Because each transition from one phase to the next involves a greater commitment of resources and a decreasing irreversibility in the decisions, top management closely monitors transitions from the screening of project ideas to project conception, from conception to detailed planning, from planning to execution, and from execution to full operationalization.

Top managers structure the rules that guide the decision on when, under what conditions, and how transitions should take place. Furthermore, they make sure that all the necessary support is provided to the teams that inherit a project. This leads to a concern with integration of the various phases of a project, as well as integration with operational activities that need to be carried out simultaneously. Declerck (5) had concluded that the management of integration was, together with the management of current operations and of projects, one of the three functions of strategic management. In his analysis, he differentiated between static integration—concerned with the coexistence of management systems and the cultures associated with projects, operations, and dynamic integration—concerned with the transition of a project to a stable and profitable operation.

Interface with Key Stakeholders. Some interfaces, critical to a project's success, simply cannot be delegated. For example, in response to a trend among larger manufacturing firms to cut significantly their engineering staffs and to rely on outside consultants, some senior executives make it a point to meet periodically with a contact person in the consulting firm "to avoid surprises and keep the pressure on."

Management Development. Performance in project management is used as a criterion to identify good managers. Top managers pursue different strategies to achieve similar objectives. Some provide project managers with considerable autonomy, while others deliberately provide fewer resources than required to see how the manager deals with that constraint (test abilities). In one particular company, the president developed a compensation scheme and a promotion policy that rewarded people for submitting and sponsoring project ideas. The only way to obtain increased authority and power in that organization was through the submission of good project ideas.

Control and Monitoring. In major international engineering projects, some firms have found it essential to agree with all parties involved on the selection of outside auditors and on a schedule for project evaluations. This approach provides top management with an objective assessment of project progress and, at the same time, with a weapon to resolve potential conflicts with partners or clients alike. In companies that call on outside consultants for the conception of a project, top management has periodic meetings with a representative from the consulting firm. In one company, top management required that the consultant firm commit to assigning the same executive for the duration of the projects.

Thus, top managers are involved with project management activities within their organizations in a variety of ways. The nature and amount of their involvement with a specific project will depend on a number of factors such as time available, priorities, familiarity with the project, and so on. However, we found that a limited number of project activities played a key role in shaping top managers' attention to and involvement in project activities. These are discussed next.

Project Characteristics and Project Management Methods

How do senior executives develop a portfolio of project management methods that enables their organizations to carry out successfully projects whose unique characteristics and circumstances call for specific management methods? The following project characteristics (see Table 2) were found to play a determining role in shaping top management approaches to project management:

Project Size. As the size of projects undertaken by an organization grows, so does the infrastructure required, as measured by the number of staff, number of expertise specializations involved, financial commitments, or the level of technical difficulty. Concomitantly, the projects report to increasingly higher levels within the hierarchy. In order to better respond to the unique and differing challenges posed by smaller and larger projects, some firms have implemented two different sets of project management systems. Systems that apply to small projects tend to rely on elaborate and detailed policies and procedures, while those that apply to large projects tend to rely more on broader sets of guidelines.

However, we also found that a number of the firms that discriminated between small and large projects were far more effective in managing the larger projects than the smaller ones. There is a natural tendency to pay greater attention to the larger projects, which carry greater stakes, have more visibility, and involve more resources; hence, they comprise greater risk. For example, a company in the steel industry had developed a very systematic procedure to manage major capital projects (over $100 million), but, at the same time, the same firm runs close to one thousand small ($50,000) maintenance, small improvements, and so on. These smaller projects were assigned to junior managers who derived little recognition or status from their involvement and received little top management attention and support. As the company discovered, smaller projects were plagued with delays, cost overruns, and missed deadlines with cumulative detrimental effects to the smooth operation of the organization as a whole and to the development of a strong cadre of project managers. In the end, all the benefits derived from improved large project management approaches were erased by the ineffective small project management systems. The pragmatic response was to put in place two project management systems, one for the large projects and one for the small projects.

Project Impact. The greater the impact of a project on its users-clients, the greater the need for participatory and informal management structures. In the final analysis, consistent with Slevin and Pinto (22), the success of a project can be measured by the value created through its execution on behalf of the users. Since projects inevitably bring change, it is normal to expect that the greater the change, the greater the likely resistance from the user-client. As a result, the greater the familiarity of the users-clients with the project—obtained by keeping channels of communication continuously open or by involving the users-clients in all phases of the project—the greater their acceptance and commitment. Project management is a political process indeed, hence, the need to involve key stakeholders in the decisions that affect them. This is particularly true at the project design stage.

Project Ambiguity. The greater the ambiguity and uncertainty in a project's objectives and functions, the greater the need for feedback mechanisms at shorter intervals for increased speed of experimentation, the breaking up of the project into smaller phases to allow for partial modifications of reversibility, incremental approaches, and intensive communications.

Project Complexity. Project complexity impacts the degree of modularization and the degree of centralization appropriate to its successful management. The analysis of project management practices in the organizations studied has highlighted two important dimensions of project complexity: complexity in project structure and complexity in project execution.

Dealing simultaneously with these two dimensions can create conflicting demands for top management. On the one hand, the greater the complexity in structure, measured by the number of elements constituting a project, the greater the pressure to break the original objective into multiple subsystems and, therefore, to decentralize the management of each module. On the other hand, the greater the complexity in execution, measured by the complexity of the interactions between the elements constituting the project, the greater the need for quick dissemination of information, for quality communications and, therefore, for centralization. Achieving a manageable balance between these conflicting pressures requires considerable judgment and skill.

Project Position in the Life Cycle. The data from our case studies confirm previous empirical findings that time is the best dimension on which to structure the observation, analysis, and management of projects. Since each phase of a project (identification, conception, execution, and termination) has a unique set of objectives and conditions, each phase implies a unique combination of key tasks implemented by a different set of focal actors, according to a distinct process that defines the sequence in which these tasks need to be carried out. All of these are linked by a unique set of organizational arrangements and structure.

Project's Characteristics		Project Management Systems
Size	→	Infrastructure requirements: staff, outside expertise, cash flow, level of technical expertise. Hierarchical level of control
Impact	→	Greater involvement of users-clients in decision-making Need for participatory and informal structures
Ambiguity & Uncertainty	→	Need for feedback mechanisms, for increased speed of experimentation, for multiple phases to allow for partial reversibility, for incremental approaches and intensive communication
Complexity	→	Pressure to break the original objective into multiple sub-systems Need for quick dissemination of information for quality communications Need for centralization & modularization
Project Life Cycle	→	Control progress of every project Management of conflicts Management of transitions from phase to phase
Strategic Importance	→	Screening and selection of projects

Table 2   Project Management Model

All along the cycle, management monitors and controls a project's progress through careful attention to the project's scope, delays, costs, and performance levels. Management systems need to emphasize conflict resolution processes and the smooth transition, with adequate support, from phase to phase.

Project Strategic Importance. How high a project ranks on the organization's agenda often supersedes all the preceding factors in determining the amount of visibility and managerial attention it receives. Top managers may sponsor projects that do not meet the normal performance criteria (e.g., return on investment, payback) because they are deemed of strategic importance to the future wellbeing and profitability of the organization. Such projects may not follow established procedures. Typically, they require more frequent feedback to top management and are subject to different resource allocation criteria.

The project's portfolio management task is made all the more complex in that it needs to accommodate simultaneously the challenges, problems, and constraints created by multiple combinations of project characteristics such as those discussed above. Firms seem to adopt one of two pragmatic responses. In the first, a heavy emphasis is placed on the project screening process, and only projects that have been managed before are selected—the rationale being that managers can always decide not to undertake a project but cannot ignore ongoing operations.

In the second response, management can continuously adapt approaches to the circumstances created by a given combination of project characteristics. This approach, however, can prove quite ineffective as the number of projects undertaken increases.

In order to institutionalize the lessons learned about project management by the organization, managers formalize sets of policies and procedures so as to:

- Clarify the steps in the process together with the expectations relating to each step
- Improve the speed of execution so that less time is lost at each stage trying to "reinvent the wheel"
- Facilitate project monitoring and control by top management.

Next, we discuss some conclusions based on the analysis of top managers' efforts to systemize project management practices within their own organizations.

Top Management Approaches to Project Management

How far have the organizations examined taken the systematization of project management practices? The interviews led to the following observations:

- Among the seventeen organizations operating with well-established project management procedures, eleven operated with a single project management system and six with multiple systems, the majority of which had two systems (large projects versus small projects, commercial versus technical, offensive versus defensive, and so on). Managers observed that more and more organizations are acquiring, relative to their sizes, expertise in the management of large projects. However, the management of thousands of small projects is still a nightmare for many and should receive greater attention in the future. In summary, organizations tend to create two distinct project management systems—one that applies to the large projects and one to the small ones.
- Among the eight organizations where project management was said to be in crisis, four had single project management systems, and two had multiple systems. In most cases, the crisis emerged according to the same pattern. An organization, following a strategic decision, decides to undertake a new (in relation to its expertise) kind of project. Because it has been successful so far, the usual approach to project management is applied in the initial stages until the crisis arises. Management then realizes that project management methods and techniques are not readily transferable. The solution typically involves switching from one project management system to multiple systems. In the organizations examined, this was done by either recruiting an outsider with the necessary skills or by bringing in consultants. Invariably, the new pro-

ject was taken out of the mainstream of other organizational activities, given a project manager, and controlled through a different reporting system.

- Among the seven firms undergoing reorganization, four were setting up a single project management system (the first in their histories); three were setting up multiple systems, as they were coming out of crises.

The analysis of the project management practices in the organizations studied led us to conclude that these practices fell under one of three broad categories—rules, systems of rules, and meta-rules—and that the selection of the most appropriate approach was contingent upon two project portfolio characteristics—the number of projects and their homogeneity. Let us examine these two conclusions in turn.

Rules, Systems of Rules, and Meta-Rules

Although no two projects are alike, all projects share a number of common characteristics that form the foundation of the systematization of project management methods and techniques in a single body of knowledge. The data for our study suggest that, in practice, at any given time, a limited number of variables appear to shape the general approaches to project management adopted by an organization. These are the number and the homogeneity of projects undertaken. These two factors determine the appropriateness of one of four project management methods:

- Ad hoc approaches
- Detailed rules and procedures
- Various systems of rules and procedures
- Meta-rules (see Figure 1).

The following typology of project management methods results:

When few projects are undertaken, learning is impeded or impossible. Thus, in such cases, project management systems are commonly imported (subcontracted to an engineering consulting firm or duplicated from another firm by, for example, hiring a project manager from a competitor) or simply created by an individual with organizational project management capabilities.

When a large number of relatively homogeneous projects are undertaken, it becomes possible to specify and apply effectively detailed rules and procedures applicable to all projects. In such cases, project management manuals can be prepared and are extremely useful. In this scenario, project management becomes an exercise in administration where strict adherence to the system is expected and required.

When many heterogeneous projects are undertaken, top managers have two options—create homogeneous subgroups or define meta-rules. If they classify the projects into homogeneous subgroups, they develop a standardized system for each segment of the project portfolio. This brings us back to the preceding

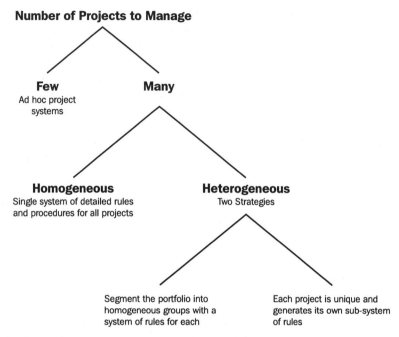

Number of Projects to Manage

Few
Ad hoc project
systems

Many

Homogeneous
Single system of detailed rules
and procedures for all projects

Heterogeneous
Two Strategies

Segment the portfolio into
homogeneous groups with a
system of rules for each

Each project is unique and
generates its own sub-system
of rules

Figure 1 Typology of Project Management Systems

case but multiplied by the number of groups constituted. Thus, project management methods can be classified as independent systems of rules and procedures. Each system, relevant to its own set of circumstances, is implemented within the organization's overall strategic constraints and is, therefore, subject to the strategic priorities set by top management and their resulting tradeoffs. In this regard, a distinct challenge for top management is the integration of the various groups, each characterized by its own project culture and idiosyncrasies.

Alternatively, when the many heterogeneous projects cannot be classified into homogeneous categories, top managers need to define meta-rules, i.e., rules that generate their own system of rules and procedures in response to the specific and unique circumstances surrounding each project.

The notion of a global directive, or meta-rule, is replacing that of detailed procedures. It has led to a new management style founded on the utilization of general guidelines implemented by autonomous project managers wholly accountable for a project's success. In this system, a project manager needs to interpret and apply the guidelines to the unique circumstances of a project. The manager's performance is then assessed by an independent corporate audit team whose main responsibilities are to ensure that all guidelines have been followed and to assess the quality of the project manager's judgment in adapting them to a project.

Spie Batignolles was the first company in our research to make public the replacement of voluminous manuals of procedures by a new set of guidelines presented in pocket diary format. The implementation of the new project management philosophy had been triggered by the difficulty of applying procedures to projects for which they had not been designed. Following an era of unending revisions, each revision leading to its own revision, and so forth, the size of the project management manuals had become so monumental and so inversely proportional to their usefulness that senior management questioned their existence. The seventeen rules for successful project management contained in the booklet were derived from an in-depth review of over a hundred successful and unsuccessful projects.

In practice, the larger organizations tend to rely on a system where a combination of approaches coexist to better respond to the specific needs, constraints, and challenges of various segments of the portfolio and projects, all at different stages in their life cycles.

Conclusion

The development of project management practices and concepts is at a historical turning point. It is now clear that project management technology needs to be embedded in an organization's strategic management system. Because this conclusion has been reached at the same time by two currents of thought— namely project management and strategic management, both grounded on management practice but starting from very different perspectives and premises—its power and relevance are all the more convincing.

On the one hand, the discipline of project management moved from a narrow to a broader concept embodied in the *PMBOK Guide*, which explicitly recognizes the existence of a professional body of knowledge pertaining to project management that applies across all types of projects. On the other hand, the discipline of strategic management is finding that the formulation and implementation of strategies creates a need to integrate a sound understanding of how to manage strategic projects and, even further, each and every project.

In an increasingly competitive world, project management competence is emerging as a key success factor of the same magnitude and with the same potential impact as the marketing function had in the fifties. Project management is no longer in its infancy. However, it is not yet a mature discipline either. Better and more refined models need to be developed to explain project success and failure and, therefore, to improve project management practice. The integration of project management practice into a strategic management framework is an important step in that direction.

Appendix

Sample Questions for the Interviews

- Is project management recognized and treated as a specific activity in your organization?
- Does your organization have specific procedures to guide you in developing, analyzing, and executing projects? If so, how formalized are they?
- In what circumstances were those procedures implemented? Through what process?
- Do these procedures vary according to the kinds of projects they are applied to?
- What are the key success factors for the kinds of projects your organization undertakes?
- What are the obstacles to successful projects? To successful project management?

Survey Design

Respondents were asked to provide background information about their organizations (size, sector of activity, rating of the effectiveness of their project management systems, number of projects undertaken in a year, size of those projects, and so on).

Then, they were asked to indicate who (board of directors, executive committee, president, vice president, division manager, and so on) was involved at what stage of a project's life cycle. Each phase was broken down into specific activities, e.g., for the planning phase:

- Generating project ideas
- Taking ideas to proposal stage
- Screening project ideas
- Approving project start-up
- Formulating performance objectives
- Setting project schedules
- Formulating budgets
- Establishing resource allocation rules
- Identifying the project team, and so on.

References

1. Avots, I. 1975. Making Project Management Work—The Right Tools for the Wrong Project Managers. *Advanced Management Journal* 4, no. 4: 20–26.

2. Bilden, T., and H. Hiorth. 1984. The Scandinavian Alternative to Project Management. *AACE Transactions*: 1–6.

3. Burgelman, R. 1984. Managing the Internal Corporate Venturing Process. *Sloan Management Review* (Winter): 33–48.

4. Cooper, R. 1975. *Why New Products Fail.* Industrial Marketing Management, Elsevier Scientific Publishing Company: 315–326.

5. Declerck, R., P. Eymery, and M.A. Crener. 1980. Le Management Strategique des Projets. *Editions Hommes et Techniques.*

6. Declerck, R., J.P. Debourse, and C. Navarre. 1982. Methode de Direction Generale. *Editions Hommes et Techniques.*

7. Greiner, L., and V. Schein. 1981. The Paradox of Managing a Project-Oriented Matrix: Establishing Coherence Within Chaos. *Sloan Management Review* (Winter): 17–22.

8 Henry, D. 1977. Systems Project Management—A Snap. *Journal of Systems Management* 28, no. 2: 33–35.

9. Jacobs, R. 1972. Putting Manage into Project Management. *Journal of Systems Management* 23, no. 1: 20.

10. Jonason, P. 1971. Project Management Swedish Style. *Harvard Business Review* 49, no. 6: 104.

11. Kerzner, H. 1980. Evaluation Techniques in Project Management. *Journal of Systems Management* 31, no. 2: 10–19.

12. Kottcamp, E.H., and B. Rushton. 1979. Stimulating Technological Innovation—Improving the Corporate Environment. *Research Management* (November): 19–22.

13. Meredith, J., and S. Mantel. 1985. *Project Management: A Managerial Approach.* John Wiley and Sons, Inc.

14. Navarre, C., and J.L. Schaan. 1987. International Engineering Project Management: Key Success Factors in a Changing Industry. *International Journal of Project Management* 5, no. 4: 238–245.

15. Olsen, R. 1981. Can Project Management Be Defined? *A Decade of Project Management.* Project Management Institute: 18-19.

16. Stardeli, G. 1975. Project Management—Controlling Uncertainty. *Journal of Systems Management* 26, no. 5: 28–29.

17. Venuti-Anthonty, J., and Robert J. Campbell. 1980. 20 Practical Guidelines to Project Management. *Modern Materials Handling* 35, no. 2: 80–81.

18. Walsh, M. 1978. Common Sense in Project Management. *Journal of Systems Management* 29, no. 5: 13–19.

19. White, W. 1977. Effective Transfer of Technology from Research to Development. *Research Management* (May): 30–34.

20. Wolff, M. 1984. Rules of Thumb for Project Management. *Research Management* 27, no. 4: 11–13.

21. Youker, R. 1981. Organizational Alternatives for Project Management. *A Decade of Project Management.* Project Management Institute: 141–147.

22. Slevin, Dennis P., and Jeffrey K. Pinto. 1986. The Project Implementation Profile: New Tool for Project Managers. *Project Management Journal* (September): 52–70.

Organizational Culture and Project Leader Effectiveness

Michael Elmes, Innovation Management Program,
School of Management, Syracuse University
David Wilemon, Innovation Management Program,
School of Management, Syracuse University

Project Management Journal 19, no. 4 (September 1988)

I N THE PAST FIVE YEARS, corporate culture and its influence on organizations has been the focus of significant research and study. Scholars are now examining the implications of this research for managers who operate within a particular culture or set of cultures. Some managers might be described as "culture reactors." Through lack of experience and awareness they are often controlled by the norms and values of their cultures and see few opportunities to influence or change them. They also have difficulty understanding and adapting to differing norms and values across a variety of organizational cultures. By contrast, managers who are "culturally proactive" have strong feelings for their organization's culture—a deeper awareness about how it shapes behavior. These same managers are more sensitive to and capable of interacting with other kinds of cultures as well. This sensitivity makes them more adaptive, flexible, creative, and effective.

Focus

The purpose of our article is to help project managers better understand cultural processes, identify culture types, and develop ways for recognizing, changing, and adapting to their own organizations and that of their clients. Such knowledge can help project managers become more effective.

Unlike many other types of managers, project managers often must deal with several different cultures. A project manager may have to interact with 1) the parent of a "host" organization, 2) subcultures in various departments (e.g., marketing and research and development), 3) external client groups, and 4) her own project team. Thus, awareness of culture helps project managers "read" as well as "speak" the language of the surrounding culture. This communication skill helps them develop plans, strategies, and visions that are more likely to be understood and accepted. Equally important, awareness helps managers bypass practices that violate the norms and values a culture prizes; e.g., manufacturing often values a hierarchical orientation. Finally, understanding culture can enable project managers to develop and manage their teams more effectively. Such knowledge is particularly important when project teams face indifference, hostility, or pressure about the team's mission.

Our article first examines what "culture" is and how it influences behavior. Second, it identifies and describes culture types and characteristics. Third, it looks at various methods for identifying and responding to culture types. Finally, we will discuss countercultures and their impact on organizations. Though rooted in theory, this article is prescriptive and offers several suggestions that can help project managers understand the importance of their cultural milieu more clearly.

Organizational Culture and Project Management

Sathe (27) defines "culture" as the set of assumptions, often unstated, that members of an organization share. Smirchich and Stubbart describe it as, "the degree to which a set of people share many beliefs, values and assumptions that encourage them to make mutually reinforcing interpretations of their own acts and the acts of others" (30, p. 727). Through a system of shared norms, beliefs, values, and assumptions, culture can bond individuals to each other, thereby creating shared meanings.

Sathe notes that an individual becomes committed to organizational beliefs when "he or she internalizes them, that is, when the person comes to hold them as personal beliefs or values" (30, p. 12). Because these assumptions are internalized and reinforced by experience, they may be outside an individual's awareness. Internalization most likely occurs when "he or she derives personal satisfaction from the content of the behavior because it is congruent with corresponding personal beliefs and values" (30, p. 12).

Purpose of Culture

Culture creates social ideals that guide individual behavior (14). These ideals are accomplished in a number of ways. First, culture can generate commitment to management values (16). Harrison (7) attributes the strong culture of many high-performing organizations to the close alignment of individual goals and values with organizational purposes. Strong cultures also have more influence than weak ones over how individuals interpret cues.

Second, culture can convey messages about the organization and what it stands for to insiders and outsiders in clear and often impactful ways (3). When a set of shared assumptions is present, organizations spend less time supervising,

116

training, and "managing" employees. Along similar lines, organizations learn to rely on clients and customers by observing and understanding what really matters to the organization and to its members. Last, culture serves to control, monitor, and, generally, process beliefs and behavior by manipulating the "assumptions or definitions of the situation which are taken as given by the organizational participants" (32, p. 84). Culture helps by highlighting those individuals who demonstrate as well as those who deviate from the dominant cultural norms of the organization.

How Culture Is Communicated

Culture is transmitted in two ways: directly and symbolically. Managers and supervisors directly communicate values, beliefs, and norms through policy manuals, training sessions, and informal discussions. Direct communication shapes how individuals react to situations by specifying certain perceptions, decisions, behaviors, and attitudes.

The symbolic communication of values also can be a powerful method for sharing organizational values. A symbol is a sign that means something more than itself—it is something that is invested with a particular, subjective meaning (20). Though symbols are indirect, Dandridge notes that they can act as "evocative devices for rousing, channeling and domesticating powerful emotions" (3, p. 166). One need only consider a variety of symbols—e.g., a national flag, the XEROX logo, the skull and crossbones, and the IRS—to appreciate how much feeling symbols can evoke.

There are several methods for transmitting symbols. According to Boje, Fedor, and Rowland (1), myths allow organizations to attribute meaning to activities and events. Myths enable an organization to legitimize its actions, conceal its interests, and "explain and create cause and effect relationships under conditions of incomplete knowledge" (1, p. 18). The authors cite the "big car" myth of the sixties and seventies: American automobile manufacturers "believed" that consumers only wanted big cars. Concurrently, they designed and sold inferior smaller cars, using poor sales and consumer dissatisfaction to substantiate the myth.

Storytelling is one way to introduce "myths" to an organization. According to Mitroff and Kilman (19), autobiographies of corporate leaders are a rich source of myth-making material. Frequently highlighting the "right stuff" for survival and success, such stories spread through the organization and become myths which "perpetuate corporate traditions and ... [are] used to indoctrinate new employees" (19, p. 190). A story's authenticity is often not as important as its capacity to communicate essential values, which motivate and influence others. Deal and Kennedy (4) note that many corporate myths are told during company training programs. The informal conveyance of stories also is important. Organizational rituals are defined as formal and customarily repeated acts that convey basic norms and values throughout the organization. Deal and Kennedy (4) suggest that all organizations have rituals that they repeat continually. Strong cultures use rituals to transmit meanings clearly and effectively. Weak cultures do not convey desired meanings through rituals. The authors describe a capital equipment producer when one fundamental value is "careful decision-making." During meetings, each individual speaks in order of corporate experience. This process emphasizes the importance of experience in making these careful decisions. By contrast, a meeting in a weak corporate culture may carry no underlying agreement on what ought to be accomplished: "People are late. They trickle in and trickle out. During the meetings there are lots of things people say that just fall through the cracks" (33, p. 105–106).

Culture and Its Relevance to Project Managers

Having presented an overview of culture, we now explore why an understanding of culture is important to project managers. As noted, project managers must interact with an array of cultural systems, often simultaneously. Project managers who are not aware of cultural influences often encounter conflict and misunderstandings when they deal with diverse functional departments, client groups, and even their own teams. Frequently rooted in value differences, conflicts can arise from problems in communicating across cultures. The language spoken in a research and development department may have very different meanings and interpretations than that spoken in a marketing department that wants results "yesterday."

Though some conflicts are unavoidable, many can be minimized by understanding the cultural frames of reference in which groups operate. It is important to make a concerted effort to speak and listen in ways that take these differences into account. A headstrong, reactive approach that attributes project obstacles to another person's "failures" or "stubbornness" may polarize differences, escalate conflict, and make it difficult or impossible to complete the project.

Culture Types and Characteristics

Loveinger (13) states that "every classification is an injustice." Individuals, groups, departments, and organizations seldom fit neatly into classification systems; some are complex mixtures of many cultural patterns while others may be in transition and difficult to label. Nevertheless, researchers have developed models that identify some systematic processes that organizational members use to make "sense" of their environments. Jones (9) calls these processes "axes of bias." This article will present and focus on a culture model, an archetypal model that can be helpful in understanding the different dimensions of culture.

The Jungian Framework for Understanding Culture

According to Jung, there are four psychological functions "by which consciousness obtains its orientation to experience" (10, p. 61). In decision-making, Jung maintained that "feeling" individuals tend to make judgments on the basis of whether or not something is pleasing or distasteful. "Thinking" individuals are inclined to connect ideas and use reason in making decisions. Likewise, in information gathering, individuals tend to be either "sensing" or "intuiting." "Sensing" individuals use their sensory organs to collect information and can usually point outward to the source of the information; when asked how they know something is true, an "intuiting" individual might respond, "I feel it in my bones." In integrating the above, Jung claimed that individuals tend to combine an information-gathering preference (sensing or intuiting) to make sense of and act on information.

At the organizational level, Mitroff (18) found the Jungian framework useful to "shed insight on organizational and institutional differences." Just as individuals collect information and make decisions in various ways (sensing-feeling, sensing-thinking, intuiting-feeling, intuiting-thinking), groups of individuals or organizations also create cultures based on these same (Jungian) dimensions. On the decision-making dimension, cultures that are feeling-based tend to be flexible and innovative, and those that are thinking-based tend to be ordered, structured, and rational. On the information-gathering dimension, cultures that are sensing-based tend to focus on internal concerns and be short-term oriented; intuition-based cultures tend to focus on external concerns and be more long-term oriented. Cameron (2) does an excellent job of building a more descriptive model based upon Mitroff's earlier work. He notes the following:

> Organizational culture consists of the shared interpretations and
> assumptions of organizational members. Cues are generated and
> reinforced in organizations that lead individuals to a common
> view. ... Organizational cultures often emphasize one end of the
> continua more than the other end which leads to a shared set of
> assumptions and viewpoints.

Cameron labels the four different culture types as Clan, Market, Hierarchy, and Adhocracy (see Figure 1). A brief description of the leadership style bases for bonding (or "glue") and strategic concerns of each are provided. In the next section we will use Cameron's classification scheme to examine four different culture types potentially important to project managers (2).

Identifying Characteristics of Culture

Having presented a model of culture based upon archetypal understructures, we exemplify these culture types. We will, then, hypothesize likely characteristics with regard to physical appearances, myths and stories, rituals, and decision-making

Figure 1   A Model of Organizational Culture Types

styles. These characteristics should be regarded as possible cultural traits based upon the model.

Clan Culture—Intel Corporation

The clan culture emphasizes flexibility in its decision-making style and an internally oriented approach to information collection. Ouichi's (22) description of the Intel Corporation provides an excellent example of an organization dominated by a clan culture. The key features of Intel's culture are cooperation, collective responsibility, and consensus decision-making. Teams are a critical part of the work environment, and accomplishing team objectives is valued more highly than accomplishing individual objectives. Intel's new buildings are designed to have an excess of conference rooms (each with blackboards) so that individuals can meet informally (24, p. 220). Managers are encouraged to share information with each other (even MBO results), criticize each other's work, and open decision-making to all levels of the organization, including the lowest. Like other clan cultures, Intel believes in long-term employment and tries to reassign, rather than release, individuals who face career development problems.

The founders of the company—Robert Noyce, Andrew Grove, and Gordon Moore—purposefully placed the cultural emphasis on teamwork and cooperation. They run the corporation as a team. As mentors for the culture, they take an active role in teaching new employees about the organization (2). For example, Intel President Andrew Grove states that his new-hire orientation teaching is his most significant contribution to the company (23, p. 343).

Intel typifies the clan culture's member-oriented approach to running an organization. In such a culture one is likely to find the following characteristics.

Physical Appearance: Groups of people working together; offices designed to minimize structural barriers to communication; offices and hallways warmly decorated; slogans emphasizing teamwork; informal dress and attire.

Myths and Stories: Themes of cooperation, participation, and mutual respect; focus on internally overcoming organizational problems; emphasis on traits and qualities of the founders (mentors).

Rituals: Gaining information and ideas from all levels of the organization; long meetings; company-sponsored social events, parties and activities; health and day care facilities.

Decision-Making Style: Much collaboration before decisions are made; once made, rapid commitment of resources to implement plans.

Market Culture—Proctor and Gamble (P&G)

In contrast to Intel's clan culture, we suggest that P&G is an example of a culture with a market orientation. By "market," we mean cultures that are oriented, primarily, toward the external environment (2). These organizations often use highly structured analytical processes in decision-making.

During the past fifty years, few companies have had P&G's record for introducing successful new products. One of the reasons P&G succeeds is its emphasis on competition, achievement, and quality. According to *Forbes* magazine (5, p. 33), P&G planned direct frontal attacks on General Foods in the coffee business, on Tampax in the tampon business, on American Hospital Supply and J&J in the disposable medical gown business, on Coca Cola and Pepsico in soft drinks, and on Ralston Purina in pet foods, among others. According to P&G Chairman Edward Harness, any kind of household products that could be mass-produced and sold for low cost in food, drug, and variety stores was fair game for P&G.

The hero of the competitive market system at P&G is the brand manager. "Time and again the system of myths and tales lauds the valiant brand manager who has challenged those many years his senior and repositioned his brand against all odds" (24, p. 213). Part of this hero-making process at P&G is the internal competition among the brand managers themselves. Peters and Waterman note that "a large share of new P&G products is likely attributable to the intensity of the brand managers' desire to be judged 'winners.' Each year's brand managers become a 'class' and competition among classes is 'fierce'" (24, p. 217).

The following characteristics of market cultures are often observed.

Physical Appearance: Individuals dress conservatively but sharply, in order to "stand out"; individuals move quickly, giving the sense of being constantly "on the go"; offices emphasize status and success over comfort and relaxation.

Myths and Stories: Often focus on product successes and victories; may include stories about individual "stars" who, through hard work and persuasion, were able to accomplish the "impossible"; may also deal with vanquishing the competition.

Rituals: Play hard/work hard (4); publicly recognizable rewards (promotions, pay increases); constant monitoring of the competition; senior management involvement in highly valued activities (e.g., executives making sales calls).

Decision-Making Style: Market-driven, rational, and oriented toward "facts," particularly facts about the market, competition, and costing. Decisions based on expertise and/or personal track records rather than the rank or position of the person in the organization.

Hierarchical Culture—"Meridian Telephone Company"

A third culture type takes a hierarchical or bureaucratic form. In a bureaucracy, individuals look internally for relevant information and use an orderly, rational decision-making process (2). Much has been written about bureaucratic organizations. Mintzberg (17) states that bureaucracies build complex administrative systems in order to regulate and oversee the highly specialized work of the operating core. These administrative systems help "keep the lid on conflicts that inevitably result from the alienation that goes with routine, circumscribed jobs" (1, p. 98). Control and power over policy and decision-making are concentrated in a few individuals at the top. Information from the outside environment frequently enters the organization at the bottom or middle of the hierarchy and is "filtered" as it moves up the organization. The combination of limited information and a rigid, hierarchical structure makes it difficult for planners in bureaucracies to identify and respond to environmental change.

Bureaucracies are common among large manufacturing companies, as well as among service industries such as insurance companies, utilities, and railroads. They also are characteristic of government agencies, which, like regulated industries, are careful of their actions and likely to formalize their operating processes.

Kanter (11) uses the example of a telephone company she calls "Meridian Telephone" to depict a bureaucratic culture. At Meridian there were fifteen levels of managers, each with finely specialized duties. Very few managers crossed organizational lines to work or even communicate with other managers. Information was guarded rather than shared. A decision, for example, to purchase new computer equipment required the approval of several different parties, each with their own issues and agendas (many having little or no bearing on the intended uses of the equipment).

Hierarchical or bureaucratic cultures often have the following identifying characteristics.

Physical Appearance: Many clerical and other staff members doing repetitive tasks; conservative dress and décor (individualism in dress or décor can be "threatening" to the hierarchical chain of command); pictures of organizational leaders on walls; feeling of orderliness and routine.

Myths and Stories: Themes such as: being a "team player" (i.e., fitting in, conforming); a deference for authority; loyalty to the organization; emphasis on the organization's infallibility, historical greatness, longevity, and experience.

Rituals: Formal: meetings, meetings, meetings; informal: maneuvering for resources, building coalitions to increase "clout" or block competing projects; "status effect": telling superiors what one thinks they want to hear rather than reveal what is really happening.

Decision-Making Style: Slow and time consuming (must go through many levels), decisions may be based on constituent influence rather than on worth; unpredictable; decisions at one level can be, and often are, overturned at high levels.

Adhocracy Culture—Minnesota Mining and Manufacturing (3M)

A fourth culture type is an adhocracy. Somewhat like clan cultures, adhocracies are flexible and feeling-oriented in how they make and implement decisions. Like the market culture, they are oriented toward the external environment in their information processing. In direct contrast to bureaucracies, adhocracies are innovative and entrepreneurial. They are more loosely structured, able to adapt quickly to changing environments, and very successful at introducing new, usually high technology, products to the marketplace (2).

One example of an "adhocracy" is 3M. At 3M the "eleventh commandment" states, "Thou shalt not kill a new idea." In fact, at 3M, the burden of proof for any new idea is on the people who wish to disprove the idea's value (24, p. 227). Roberts notes, from his observations, that "its difficult to talk ten minutes to a janitor at 3M without the conversation turning to new products" (26, p. 134). He attributes some of this environment to the result of "promoting top management from within, frequently from successes in venture management" (26, p. 134).

A number of other factors influence 3M's innovative culture. Often, there is an executive champion who protects young workers and their projects from interference by the corporate staff. This is similar to the role of the sage or mentor in the clan culture. Also, new ventures may have access to multiple sources of capital within the company. A project leader, for example, can look for funding from a variety of sources: his own department, other departments, and the new product development department. Next, venture teams at 3M are full time, yet indefinite assignments are taken by people from a variety of backgrounds who volunteer. Because no one is involuntarily assigned to a venture team, commitment to the venture is high. A new product's success is not measured against some minimum "promised" (26, p. 136) sales volume but on how well the product performs after it has been on the market for a while. Last, in terms of rewards, both the team and the individual get promoted and/or compensated as a result of the new product's growth and sales.

The following identifying characteristics of adhocracies are frequently noted.

Physical Appearance: Focus on interpersonal communication, group decision-making, and problem solving; greater awareness of the external environment *and* the future—may make great use of charts and graphs to orient employees to the influences. Dress and décor are relaxed (to maximize employee comfort) but professional (to maintain outward professional appearance).

Myths and Stories: Frequently have these themes: cooperation, teamwork, "overcoming the odds" (internal orientation), product success, discovering product niches (external orientation).

Rituals: Repeating of the innovation process day in and day out; creating, "selling," adopting, and implementing new ideas at all levels of the organization; analyzing the market and the competition; attacking a market niche; redesigning and modifying ideas, demonstrating patience, flexibility, and the judicious use of resources.

Decision-Making Style: Collaborative, focused on the future, based on expertise of the decision-makers and on market considerations.

Identifying Culture Types

We have defined culture, its functions, and how it is communicated. We also have presented a cultural typology with specific organizational examples. This information can be used for identifying one's own culture and the cultures of other groups and organizations. Because of the variety of organizations and groups with which project managers must interact, careful analysis of different cultures can prove highly useful. In this section, we offer suggestions on how project managers can effectively identify various culture types. These suggestions are based on data collecting and conclusion making—important processes for identifying and relating different culture types.

Data Collecting. When a project manager meets a new culture, she should be as open as possible to the immediate, concrete experience. Sensory (sights, sounds, touches, and so on) and intuitive processes ("hunches") can be used to collect information about the culture. Questions—"What are the physical surroundings like? How do people interact with one another? What kinds of stories do I hear? What values and concerns are espoused? How would I feel if I worked in this environment?—can help the project manager collect and organize enough information to draw initial conclusions about the culture. These insights also can become the basis for developing effective influence strategies.

Conclusion-Making. On the basis of experience and reflection, the project manager draws conclusions about the culture. While open-minded observation was important in the data collecting stage, in the conclusion-making stage a project manager needs to use analytical skills to derive generalizations from his experience. For example, the project manager may decide that the client group is "clan-like" or the research and development department has strong, "adhocratic" characteristics.

Strategies for Managing Cultures

Having derived generalizations about culture types, a project manager can now experiment with these generalizations. In so doing, the project manager develops an "influence strategy." The strategies discussed here are based, in part, on Lynch's (15) application of Grave's (6) human value system to organizational culture. They represent guidelines, which the managers can use to improve communication across cultural and functional barriers. The strategies discussed here also rely on Thomas and Kilmann's (1974) matrix of behavioral preferences. It is important for project managers to experiment with such strategies but not be limited by them.

Discussed below are examples of our types of cultures. For each culture we hypothesize ways that the project leader can more effectively adapt to the values and norms of each culture.

Clan Culture

Because clan cultures are highly participative, it is essential to focus on consensus building. A project manager in a clan culture can create a "critical mass" of support by encouraging many key people to participate in the project. Listening, expressing concern, and communicating trust are important in helping people make a real commitment to the project. Project managers can trace such steps as equalizing pay, allowing alternative work schedules (flextime), and minimizing destructive competition within the team (15, p. 63).

Like other aspects of the clan culture, conflicts are handled by working together. "Collaborating" combines assertive and cooperative behaviors. It involves digging into an issue to identify the underlying concerns and finding alternatives that meet the concerns of the conflicting parties (31). When conflicts arise in a clan culture, it is important to express one's point of view and make real efforts to cooperate, avoiding "heavy handedness" or coercion. In such situations, the project manager can listen carefully to the concerns of others to build a consensus for resolution.

Market Culture

Since the market culture is highly competitive and future oriented, project managers need to devote their energies toward task completion. To achieve their goals, project managers may help team members and others see career opportunities, personal advancements, and other rewards for project assistance.

Because power and status are important in this culture, it may be useful to attract the direct or indirect support of "stars" or heroes" of the culture. A "management by objective" approach is well accepted in this culture. Unlike the clan culture, which emphasizes close interpersonal relationships, members of a market culture value economic growth and good functional relationships.

In a market culture, competition is one of the principal means by which individuals attempt to resolve conflicts. This mixture of assertiveness and competitiveness reflects a "win-lose" orientation. Project managers in a market culture will attempt to find ways to come out "on top," either by getting the support of high status individuals within the culture or by promoting the project as a market share builder or career booster.

Hierarchical Culture

Since this culture is oriented toward rules, authority, and specialized roles, project managers working in or with bureaucracies are usually the most successful if they use "appropriate channels" and communicate in a precise, detailed manner. It is important to allow enough time for requests and information to be processed. To garner the required support, it may be necessary to "trade something" with other groups. It is also useful to appeal to the culture's strong sense of tradition, which is readily available within many long-lived bureaucracies. Nontraditional or innovative approaches to managing projects can create major obstacles between the organizational culture and project managers. Because the culture often suppresses creativity, it is important to follow the path of what Schein (28) calls "creative individualism": adherence to the core values of the culture (ends, e.g., what it manufactures) but creativity with the secondary values (means, e.g., manufacturing processes).

The dominant conflict resolution pattern in bureaucracies is avoidance. Avoidance usually combines unassertive behavior with an uncooperative attitude: directly opposite the clan's conflict-handling method. Avoidance may take the form of "diplomatically sidestepping an issue, postponing an issue until a better time, or simply withdrawing from a threatening situation" (25, p. 66). Because of strong resistance to change in bureaucracies, avoidance is a typical response when conflict does arise. By being sensitive to timing issues and using private communication, a project manager can create a "face-saving structure" that permits interested parties to express underlying feelings and issues, avoid public "airing" of the dispute, and move closer to conflict resolution.

Adhocracy Culture

In contrast to the use of "proper" authority channels in bureaucracies, adhocracies have relatively weak channels of authority. Consequently, project managers need to be creative and flexible in gaining support for their ideas. Project managers should provide participants with considerable freedom, intellectual challenge, and exposure to new and different problem-solving techniques. Since this culture resists close supervision, wasted time, and resources (15, p. 63), project managers need to focus the "task" sensitively and provide personal autonomy and growth. Similar to the clan culture, collaboration is the dominant method of problem solving and conflict resolution.

Creating a Team Culture

Just as an organization culturally transmits its values to its members, so a team creates a culture through which it transmits values to its members. Mower and Wilemon (21) describe team building as a process aimed at developing a team's task competencies (meeting goals, objectives, and targets) and interpersonal competencies (resolving conflicts, listening, and building trust). An effective team culture teaches members to develop these competencies fully. This team-building process advances through a series of phases to reach a level of high, sustained performance. Table 1 displays qualities teams need to learn in order to become effective and perform at a high, sustained level.

Project managers can help teams reach high performance levels in two ways. First, they can buffer most of the interference that the team might encounter from inside and outside the organization. In *The Soul of a New Machine*, Tracy Kidder (12) characterized Tom West's primary role as sheltering his team from organizational conflicts that could impede the team's progress in its computer design-build task. Protecting the team is particularly important in situations where dominant cultural values (e.g., competition, or rules and regulations, and so on) interfere with accomplishing the project team's goals.

The second way project managers help build effective teams is through the values they transmit to team members. As in the organization, project managers transmit values both directly (through training manuals, discussions) and symbolically. For example, a project manager who wants to reduce the impact of her authority on the team might take an office far from where team members normally work, or she may encourage a highly participative team environment. Another method of transmitting values is to share different task review roles (clarifier, critical evaluator, devil's advocate) with team members on a rotating basis during project meetings.

The use of symbolic gestures by a project manager can backfire if they are inconsistent with the level of team maturity, interfere with other symbols, or are incongruent with the team leader's behavior. Smirchich (29) gives the example of a corporation that had recently acquired a new company. There was considerable friction on the executive team between the "new" outside people and the company old-timers. Because of his fear of conflict, the corporation president chose not to deal with the friction but rather to focus on cooperation. At one point, he circulated among his top managers a full-sized mounted wagon wheel with the slogan, "Wheeling Together." Instead of enhancing cooperation, the "wheel" only reinforced the current, negative working relationships that managers actually had with one another.

To better understand the interaction between team culture and development, it is worth noting the phases through which project teams progress (21). In Phase One, team members become comfortable with each other and the task. In Phase Two, members become clearer about their importance to the team and the task. In Phase Three, members focus on the execution of this task. Lastly, in Phase Four, members evaluate what they have learned and accept the completed task. At each of these phases, project managers can (1) protect the culture from specific (outside) influences and (2) communicate values that move participants to the next phase.

Consider a project team in a market culture. Typically, the individuals who make up the team will see participation on the team as an opportunity to compete with one another and get ahead. One often finds team members involved in power struggles by Phase Two. At this point, a project manager would need to communicate the importance of cooperation over competition. She might institute performance-based incentives for the team or try to change the team's frame of reference from intra-group to inter-group competition.

Countercultures

Sometimes referred to as "skunkworks," countercultures are teams or groups whose values and beliefs differ markedly from those of the general or dominant culture of the overall organization. Some countercultures are accepted—even encouraged. The organization sets them up to function with different values on new or unusual tasks. Many countercultures, however, are unsanctioned. Managers may decide that the dominant cultural values are no longer effective because of changes in the marketplace, technology, or task. Because the normal or usual way of getting things done no longer works, they choose to operate outside the norms and values that determine what and how work is accomplished.

The project manager who manages his team "against the grain" of the organization runs some risks. Sathe notes that managers who anticipate resistance to their countercultures must: "1) withdraw from the course of action and conform to the culture, 2) attempt to deviate constructively from the culture, without trying to change it, or 3) attempt to change the cultural assumptions that are involved" (27, p. 284). The first route is undesirable, and the third is difficult to accomplish.

Key Variables	Ineffective Teams	Effective Teams
Goals	Goals unstated or unclear.	Goals are clear and accepted.
Roles	Individual responsibilities are unclear.	Responsibilities are clear and change as needed.
Conflict	Conflict is suppressed, producing destructive attitudes and behaviors.	Conflict is managed openly and accepted as a vital part of team development.
Learning	Team learning is minimal.	Learning is valued and captured.
Leadership	One person is seen as the leader. Other people stuck in roles.	Leadership is seen as a shared responsibility.
Performance	Lack of concern for performance—objectives are not met.	Performance, satisfaction, and growth are valued and achieved.
Communication	Communication is guarded and restricted.	Communication is clear, open, and energetic.
Processes	Team processes emerge that may impede team progress.	Team processes are "invented"—which ensure alignment with team objectives.
People	Team members' personal and professional needs are ignored.	Individual goals are blended with team objectives.
Power	Many team members feel powerless. Power inequities cause an uneven desire to contribute.	Team members feel powerful— each one's contribution is valued and sought.

Source: J. Mower and D. Wilemon, "Team Building in a Technical Environment," in D. Kocaoglu, Editor, *Handbook of Technology Management*. 1989.

Table 1   Characteristics of Effective and Ineffective Teams

The success of "constructive deviation" depends on how successfully the project manager uses one of the following strategies. "Self-insurance" means "going against the grain on the basis of one's credibility and acceptance within the culture" (27, p. 285). The more accepted one is within the culture, the more tolerance the culture will have for movement from the norm. "Cultural-insurance" is a strategy based upon getting the support of those with high status. Sathe calls this "spreading the risk of nonconformity among the culture's 'old faithful'" (27, p. 285). "Countercultural clout" is successful if a manager gains the support of significant numbers of lower status members within the organization.

Martin and Siehl (16) attribute John DeLorean's success at creating a counterculture at General Motors to "constructive deviation." He "articulated opposing views, translated them into concrete policy, and facilitated their role implementation by personally role modeling the counterculture behavior" (27, p. 287). In addition to the support of his staff and followers, DeLorean effectively introduced successful new product lines and increased profits as a GM division manager. His success through countercultural clout and cultural insurance created the necessary momentum.

Summary

The purpose of this article has been to demonstrate that groups and organizations have unique personalities and value systems. The better a project manager understands the concept of culture, the more effective he will be in gaining support and guiding the project through the myriad or organizational mazes.

The first step is being aware of the culture (core values) and what's important to an organization and its functional groupings. The models of cultural types presented here should be helpful to project managers in terms of what to look for in cultural values and nuances. Second, project managers need to devise strategies to interact effectively with the identified culture(s). We have given several examples of strategies most likely to be successful with different cultural types. Third, it is important for project managers to recognize that each team will have its own culture. Team leaders have many opportunities to create and shape their cultures in purposeful ways. This can be an important part of the team development and climate-setting process.

We hope that more empirical research will follow our initial journey on the relationship of corporate culture to project management. We believe that organizational culture provides a fertile research area for better understanding project management and its processes.

References

1. Boje, D.M., D.B. Fedor, and K.M. Rowland. 1982. Myth-Making: A Qualitative Step in OD Interventions. *Journal of Applied Behavioral Science* 18: 17–28.

2. Cameron, K. 1984. Cultural Congruence, Strength, and Type: Relationships and Effectiveness. Working Paper No. 401. Ann Arbor, MI: The University of Michigan Graduate School of Business.

3. Dandridge, T.C. 1983. Symbols' Function and Use. In *Organizational Symbolism*, Vol. 1 of *Monographs in Organizational Behavior and Industrial Relations*, edited by L.R. Pondy et al. Greenwich, CT: Jai Press, 69–79.

4. Deal, T.F., and A.A. Kennedy. 1992. *Corporate Cultures: The Rites and Rituals of Corporate Life*. Reading, MA: Addison-Wesley Publishing, Inc.

5. Gibson, P. 1978. Proctor and Gamble: It's Got a Little Hit List. *Forbes* (March 20): 33–34.

6. Graves, C. 1972. Human Nature Prepares for a Momentous Leap. *The Futurist* (April): 72–87.

7. Harrison, R. 1983. Strategies for a New Age. *Human Resource Management* 22, no. 3 (Fall): 209–235.

8. ———. 1972. Understanding Your Organization's Character. *Harvard Business Review* (May–June): 119–128.

9. Jones, W.T. 1961. *The Romantic Syndrome: Towards a New Method in Cultural Anthropology and the History of Ideas.* The Hague: Martinus Wijhaff.

10. Jung, C.B. 1971. *Psychological Types.* Translated by Hall, R.F.C. Princeton, NJ: Princeton University Press.

11. Kanter, R.M. 1983. *The Change Masters: Innovation for Productivity in the American Corporation.* New York: Simon and Schuster.

12. Kidder, T. 1981. *The Soul of a New Machine.* New York: Avon.

13. Loveinger, J. 1977. *Ego Development: Conceptions and Theories.* New York: Jossey-Bass.

14. Louis, M.R. 1983. Organizations as Cultural Bearing Milieux. In *Organizational Symbolism*, Vol. 1 of *Monographs in Organizational Behavior and Industrial Relations,* edited by L.R. Pondy et al. Greenwich, CT: Jai Press, 39–54.

15. Lynch, D. 1984. *Your High Performance Business Brain.* Englewood Cliffs, NJ: Prentice Hall, Inc.

16. Martin, J., and C. Siehl. 1983. Organizational Culture and Counterculture: An Uneasy Symbiosis. *Organizational Dynamics* (Autumn): 52–64.

17. Mintzberg, H. 1981. Organization Design: Fashion or Fit? *Harvard Business Review* (January/February): 103–116.

18. Mitroff, I. 1983. *Stakeholders of the Organizational Mind.* San Francisco: Jossey-Bass.

19. Mitroff, I., and R. Kilman. 1976. On Organization Stories: An Approach to the Design and Analysis of Organizations Through Myths and Stories. In *The Management of Organizational Design,* edited by R.H. Kilman et al. New York: North-Holland.

20. Morgan et al. 1983. Organizational Symbolism. In *Organizational Symbolism,*Vol. 1 of *Monographs in Organizational Behavior and Industrial Relations,* edited by L.R. Pondy et al. Greenwich, CT: Jai Press, 3–35.

21. Mower, J., and D. Wilemon. 1989. Team Building in a Technical Environment. In *Handbook of Technology Management,* edited by D. Kocaoglu. New York: John Wiley.

22. Ouichi, W.G. 1981. *Theory Z: How American Business Can Meet the Japanese Challenge.* New York: Addison-Wesley.

23. Peters, T., and N. Austin. 1985. *A Passion for Excellence: The Leadership Difference.* New York: Random House.

24. Peters, T.J., and R.H. Waterman. 1982. *In Search of Excellence: Lessons from America's Best-Run Companies.* New York: Harper and Row.

25. Pneuman, R.W., and M.E. Bruehl. 1982. *Managing Conflict.* Englewood Cliffs, NJ: Prentice-Hall.

26. Roberts, E.B. 1982. New Ventures for Corporate Growth. In *The Management of Technological Innovation.* Boston: Harvard Business Review.

27. Sathe, V.1985. *Culture and Related Corporate Realities.* Homewood, IL: Richard D. Irwin, Inc.

28. Schein, E.H. 1968. Organizational Socialization and the Profession of Management. *Sloan Management Review* 9, no. 2 (Winter): 1–16.

29. Smirchich, L. 1983. Organizations as Shared Meanings. In *Organizational Symbolism*, Vol. 1 of *Monographs in Organizational Behavior and Industrial Relations,* edited by L.R. Pondy et al. Greenwich, CT: Jai Press.

30. Smirchich, L., and C. Stubbart. 1985. Strategic Management in an Enacted World. *Academy of Management Review* 10, no. 4: 724–736.

31. Thomas, K.W. Conflict and Conflict Management. In *Handbook of Industrial Psychology*, edited by M.D. Dunnette. Chicago: Rand McNally, 889–935.

32. Wilkins, A.L. 1983. Organizational Stories as Symbols. In *Organizational Symbolism,* Vol. 1 of *Monographs in Organizational Behavior and Industrial Relations,* edited by L.R. Pondy et al. Greenwich, CT: Jai Press, 81–92.

33. Wood, R.D. 1982. Rituals and Stories, Heroes and Priests. *Inc.* (December): 105–106.

PMI's Tools for Training

Project Management Casebook

Most project managers would agree that the best way to learn new concepts and techniques is to practice them as you learn them. The case study approach has proven to be an effective way to demonstrate the practical applications of project management theory, and the case studies presented in this book show you how and why projects are used in a wide variety of organizational settings in contemporary life. Fifty cases are categorized by one of following areas: planning, organizing, motivating, directing, controlling, and general.
Edited by David Cleland, Karen Bursic, Richard Puerzer, and A. Yaroslav Vlasak
ISBN: 1-880410-45-1

A Guide to the Project Management Body of Knowledge™

The basic management reference for everyone who works on projects. Serves as a tool for learning about the generally accepted knowledge and practices of the profession. As "management by projects" becomes more and more a recommended business practice worldwide, the *PMBOK™ Guide* becomes an essential source of information that should be on every manager's bookshelf. Available in hardcover or paperback, the *PMBOK™ Guide* is an official standards document of the Project Management Institute.
ISBN: 1-880410-12-5 (paperback), 1-880410-13-3 (hardcover)

Interactive PMBOK™ Guide

This CD-ROM in multimedia format makes it easy for you to access the valuable information in PMI's *A Guide to the Project Management Body of Knowledge™*. Features hypertext links for easy reference—simply click on underlined works in the text, and the software will take you to that particular section in the *PMBOK™ Guide*. Minimum system requirements: 486 PC, 8MB RAM, 10MB free disk space, CD-ROM drive, mouse or other pointing device, and Windows 3.1 or greater.

PMBOK™ Review Package

This "Box of Books" offers you a set of materials that supplements the *PMBOK™ Guide* in helping you develop a deeper understanding of the Project Management Body of Knowledge™ and helps you prepare for the PMP Certification exam. These important and authoritative publications offer the depth and breadth you need to learn more about all the *PMBOK™ Guide* knowledge areas. Includes the following titles—*Project Management: A Managerial Approach; Project Planning, Scheduling & Control; Human Resource Skills for the Project Manager; Project and Program Risk Management; Quality Management for Projects & Programs; PMBOK™ Q&A; Managing the Project Team; Organizing Projects for Success;* and *Principles of Project Management.*

Managing Projects Step-by-Step

Follow the steps, standards, and procedures used and proven by thousands of professional project managers and leading corporations. This interactive multimedia CD-ROM based on PMI's *A Guide to the Project Management Body of Knowledge™* will enable you to customize, standardize, and distribute your project plan standards, procedures, and methodology across your entire organization. Multimedia illustrations using 3-D animations and audio make this perfect for both self-paced training or for use by a facilitator.

PMBOK™ Q&A

Use this handy pocket-sized question and answer study guide to learn more about the key themes and concepts presented in PMI's international standard, *A Guide to the Project Management Body of Knowledge™*. More than 160 multiple-choice questions with answers (referenced to the *PMBOK™ Guide*) help you with the breadth of knowledge needed to understand key project management concepts.
ISBN: 1-880410-21-4

Project Management Institute Proceedings Library CD-ROM

This interactive guide to PMI's *Annual Seminars & Symposium Proceedings* offers a powerful new option to the traditional methods of document storage and retrieval, research, training, and technical writing. Contains complete paper presentations from PMI '92–PMI '97. Full text search capability, convenient on-screen readability, and PC/Mac compatibility.

Project Management Institute Publications Library CD-ROM

Using state-of-the-art technology, PMI offers complete articles and information from its major publications on one CD-ROM, including *PM Network* (1992–97), *Project Management Journal* (1992–97), and *A Guide to the Project Management Body of Knowledge™*. Offers full text search capability and indexing by *PMBOK™ Guide* knowledge areas. Electronic indexing schemes and sophisticated search engines help to find and retrieve articles quickly that are relevant to your topic or research area.

PMI Book of Project Management Forms

More than 150 actual samples and documents, used daily in the management of projects, have been compiled for you to adapt or expand upon. PMI members share forms, checklists, reports, charts, and other sample documents they use in managing their projects to make it easy for practicing project managers or students to get started or to improve their documentation. Spiral bound or CD-ROM formats available.
ISBN: 1-880410-31-1

Also Available from PMI

Principles of Project Management
John Adams et al.
ISBN: 1-880410-30-3

Organizing Projects for Success
Human Aspects of Project Management Series, Volume 1
Vijay Verma
ISBN: 1-880410-40-0

Human Resource Skills for the Project Manager
Human Aspects of Project Management Series, Volume 2
Vijay Verma
ISBN: 1-880410-41-9

Managing the Project Team
Human Aspects of Project Management Series, Volume 3
Vijay Verma
ISBN: 1-880410-42-7

Earned Value Project Management
Quentin Fleming, Joel Koppelman
ISBN: 1-880410-38-9

Value Management Practice
Michel Thiry
ISBN: 1-880410-14-1

Decision Analysis in Projects
John Schuyler
ISBN: 1-880410-39-7

ABCs of DPC
PMI's Design-Procurement-Construction Specific Interest Group
ISBN: 1-880410-07-9

How to Turn Computer Problems into Competitive Advantage
Tom Ingram
ISBN: 1-880410-08-7

The World's Greatest Project
Russell Darnall
ISBN: 1-880410-46-X

Power & Politics in Project Management
Jeffrey Pinto
ISBN: 1-880410-43-5

Best Practices of Project Management Groups in Large Functional Organizations
Frank Toney, Ray Powers
ISBN: 1-880410-05-2

Send orders to:

PMI Headquarters,
Four Campus Boulevard,
Newtown Square, Pennsylvania, 19073-3299, USA.

Or call 610-356-4600 or fax 610-356-4647.
Order online at www.pmibookstore.org